Two Essays on the Origins of Metaphysics

Two Essays on the Origins of Metaphysics

I. The Structure of Plato's Parmenides,
II. A Commentary on Aristotle's Metaphysics

Edward F. Little

Writers Club Press

San Jose   New York   Lincoln   Shanghai

Two Essays on the Origins of Metaphysics
I. The Structure of Plato's Parmenides,
II. A Commentary on Aristotle's Metaphysics

Writers Club Press
an imprint of iUniverse, Inc.

For information address:
iUniverse, Inc.
5220 S. 16th St., Suite 200
Lincoln, NE 68512
www.iuniverse.com

ISBN: 0-595-21304-9

Printed in the United States of America

PREFACE

What do you have here? Two monographs on the earliest documents of metaphysics: on a dialogue of Plato and a treatise of Aristotle. These old texts are not easy at first sight, but they do disclose their messages if you have the key. That key in each case is its structure.

Interest in metaphysics is wide and high, but some may not be serious and committed, while others may find it too "far out," too impractical, too academic. Let us be candid. This is a serious and important subject. It demands some work on your part. But it is not mysterious. If you are concerned with the nature of thought in any of its modes, or in the relation of your mind to your body and the world around it, you have reason to be interested in metaphysics.

You don't have to read Greek to learn a lot from these texts. The Greek editions by Burnet and Ross and Jaeger available from the Clarendon Press (Oxford) and by Fowler and Tredennick in the Loeb Library (Harvard) are good editions. Translations will do if you wish simply to get a decent understanding of what these are all about, but you need the Greek if you wish to argue about them, for the Greek texts are our evidence. The Loeb editions have translations on facing pages, so they are especially handy for working with both languages.

In bringing these texts to you, I have paid very little attention to modern secondary literature about them, aside from works of Werner Jaeger, Sir David Ross, Paul Moraux, Francois Lasserre, Luciano Canfora, and a very few others. One either spends huge amounts of time reading what every one has had to say about our ancient authors (and it is alot!) or one concentrates on the ancient authors themselves. I have elected to do the latter.

WARNING! The studies here would not be published now by a University Press. The ideas they contain are too new and innovative for one of those to take a chance on. They have not been "vetted" by the usual professorial jury. I am not part of that loop. On the other hand they are the product of twenty five years of careful and intense research of the two texts concerned, and they have been tried out on an audience of several hundred readers on the Internet over the last of seven years.

These studies are filled with outlines of the texts and of parts of them. The outlines are *not* intended as substitutes for reading the texts, whether in original or in translation, but as helps and guides in reading and understanding the texts. It is the texts that count. The Greek quotations are perforce printed in Roman script, in as much as the Greek script was not available on the Internet. The method of the transliteration should quickly become obvious.

EFL, Claremont, California,
December 4, 2001

THE STRUCTURE
OF PLATO'S *PARMENIDES*

CONTENTS

This is a substantial revision of an essay first completed in 1982. It is the result of work commenced with the encouragement of Philip Wheelwright in 1963. Philip was my teacher at Dartmouth College in 1938, and at the University of California (Riverside) in 1963. He died January 5, 1970 at Santa Barbara, California. I am deeply grateful for his help all those years.

References to lines in Plato's dialogues use the customary system established by Stephanus, and followed almost universally today. The reference, DK, refers to Diels-Kranz, *Die Fragmente der Vorsokratiker*, 6th edition, 1951, chapter 28 (Parmenides), section B (Fragments), also the reference system customarily used.

THE STRUCTURE OF
THE DIALOGUE AS A WHOLE

The key to the *Parmenides* is its structure. The dialogue as a whole may be divided into two parts: an introductory part, from the beginning to 137C3, and the main part, from 137C4 to the end. It is the main part, a demonstration by Parmenides, eight hypotheses about unity, that claims most of our attention. This is an intricate demonstration of dialectic that has puzzled readers for more than two thousand years. The ancient neo-platonists treated it as a metaphor, as it were, or point of departure for their quasi-religious philosophy of the One. Modern readers have considered it variously as an exercise in dialectic, as a serious philosophical exposition (with many interpretations), and as a joke.

As a work of art, as well as of philosophy, the *Parmenides* must be allowed many interpretations. This is the quality of all great works of art. Here is another interpretation, one which accepts the *Parmenides* in a straightforward manner as a serious, albeit artful, philosophical demonstration of certain important problems. It is based upon an analysis of its structure.

UNITY, BEING AND NEGATION

The *Parmenides* deals with three simple and universal human experiences, but it weaves these in a complex pattern with a weft of a fourth not-so-simple human experience. The three simple and universal experiences are: unity, being and negation.

Consider first: unity. It is an ambiguous experience for all of us. One may be a single individual, one man, one stone, one thing, one being. Or it may be an abstraction: just unity. A collection is both of these: one group of people, one heap of stones, one class of things or of beings. In short, one may be one or many.

Consider next: negation. It may mean non-existence, or it may mean otherness. To say that George Washington is not, is to deny his existence now. To say that a centaur is not, is to deny its existence ever. But to say that George Washington was not Thomas Jefferson, or that you are not I, is not to deny the existence of either (George in the past, of course), but to attribute otherness. Thus negation is either non-existence, or otherness that does exist. This is a problem that Plato took up in his dialogue, the *Sophist* (esp. 254-259). The *Sophist* has marks of being an effort to deal with two of the three experiences mentioned here, the specific combination of negation and being. Nothing had so puzzled Plato's predecessors. Here in the *Parmenides* Plato considers negation, being and unity, all three together.

Consider then thirdly: being. It may be any one being, any thing, or it may be all being, everything. It may be a particular or an abstraction. It displays the same ambiguity as unity and negation. Single palpable things, like this page, the chair you sit in, or any stick, stone or such, are well known to all of us. Their being is an obvious and common experience. But the idea of all being, the abstraction, Being, is not quite the same kind of experience. Here is the difference: we can conceive it, but it is rather difficult to be in touch with it, to perceive it, as we do individual things. Indeed, we have here the same sort of ambiguity that we encountered with unity and negation. Those too were particular and abstract, with the particularity of one thing not another, and the abstraction of absolute unity and absolute non-existence. It is just this common character of all three of these ambiguous experiences that constitutes the not-so-simple experience that we have mentioned. The ambiguity of particularity and abstraction shuttles through all three of these experiences, in all eight of the *Parmenides'* hypotheses.

PARTICULARITY AND ABSTRACTION

To reiterate, all three of the primary experiences that Plato chose to investigate in the *Parmenides* show a profound ambiguity. This ambiguity is not just a matter of human imprecision. It is rooted in the very natures of unity, being and negation, and in ourselves. It is the dichotomy of particularity and abstraction. The one may be one thing, or it may be conceptual, absolute unity. Being may refer to a particular thing, or to all being. Negation may mean not this, or not at all. Thus many may be one, what is may or may not be, and others may not be others (they may be ones). These three simple experiences, the most universal of all, turn out to be not so simple. Their ambiguity constitutes the pattern of the eight hypotheses of the *Parmenides* (137C4-166C5).

THE EIGHT HYPOTHESES

The eight hypotheses ask what happens,

> 1-2, to the one, if there is a one,
> 3-4, to the others, if there is a one,
> 5-6, to the one, if there is not a one,
> 7-8, to the others, if there is not a one.

These are the questions actually asked at the beginnings of the respective hypotheses. This conforms to the plan which Parmenides outlined in the introductory part of the dialogue (136A5-B1). If you substitute "one" for "many", and "others" for "one", making also the appropriate changes in genders of pronouns, thus reversing the viewpoint of that plan from many to one (Zeno had done just the opposite to Parmenides at the beginning of the dialogue), you have the above scheme.

At first sight this scheme appears to contain two dichotomies:

(1) being v. not-being ("there is...there is not");
hypotheses 1—4 v. 5—8;

(2) unity v. multiplicity ("one...others");
hypotheses 1, 2, 5, 6 v. 3, 4, 7, 8.

These were, to be sure, problems of primary importance to Plato and his contemporaries, but this scheme of four pairs of hypotheses also conceals the more important dichotomies of being, unity and negation. At first sight there is no suggestion of two kinds of being and unity, although there is a suggestion, if one is alert, of two kinds of negation: not-being (5, 6, 7, 8) v. otherness (3, 4, 7, 8). The two kinds of unity and being are revealed only when one analyzes the pairs, 1—2, 3—4, 5—6, 7—8, as Cornford did in 1939 (*Plato and Parmenides*). Then the abstraction and particularity of unity and being are revealed. Whereas the two kinds of negation, absolute and particular, may be seen in the abbreviated scheme given above, it takes the following expanded schemes of the eight hypotheses to reveal the ambiguities of unity and being. Strictly speaking, two schemes are necessary, since we are dealing with a protasis and an apodosis, that is an hypothesis and a conclusion, in each case. The generalized form would be: if there is (or is not) a one, what are we to say or conclude about it (or about the others)? The first scheme here refers to the protases, or hypotheses proper, i.e. the "if" clauses. The parentheses will enclose the kind of one or being that is meant in each case.

1. One	(Form)	is
2. one	(copy)	is
3. one	(copy)	is
4. One	(Form)	is
5. one	(copy)	is not
6. One	(Form)	is not
7. one	(copy)	is not
8. One	(Form)	is not

The second scheme refers to the apodoses, or conclusions: what kind of one or others is the conclusion talking about?

1. One	(Form)	is not
2. one	(copy)	is many
3. others	(copy)	are ones
4. Others	(Form)	is not one
5. One	(Form)	is
6. One/one	(Form/copy)	is not
7. others	(copy)	are
8. Others/others	(Form/copy)	are not

Or, more briefly (consolidated):

if:		then:	
1. One	is	One	is not
2. one	is	one	is many
3. one	is	others	are ones
4. One	is	Others	is not one
5. one	is not	One	is
6. One	is not	one	is not
7. one	is not	others	are
8. One	is not	Others	are not

Hypotheses six and eight deserve special comment: both Form and copy are not. Why? The text of six is clear: not-being in no way whatsoever is, nor does it in any way participate in being (163C6-7). There is no one of any kind, Form or copy. Of course, we may logically omit reference to the Form in the conclusion, since it has already been negated in the hypothesis, but we follow the text here, which is a sweeping denial of any sort of one whatsoever. The text of eight also includes a sweeping denial of the others, albeit in its own special way: they neither are, nor are conceivable. Again we may omit reference to the copy in the conclusion, if we wish, since it has been made clear: no Form, no copy (#6).

In these schemes the particularity and abstraction of unity and being, as well as of negation, are brought clearly into view. But let us take a closer look at the eight hypotheses.

Hypothesis 1 has to do with the Form of the One, or absolute or abstract Unity. Ei hen estin, allo ti ouk an eiE polla to hen, "If there is a One, the One may not be anything else [or] many." The definition of the One here is pure unity, an abstraction. Even the word "is" (estin) is extraneous, as the conclusion of this hypothesis shows (141E9—10). We could have deduced that right away, had we been alert. Plato confirms this too near the beginning of the second hypothesis (142C2-3) where he emphasizes the distinction of it from the first, distinguishing the hen hen ("One One") of the first hypothesis from the hen estin ("one is" or one that exists) of the second. Unity and being are other or many.

Hypothesis 2, having to do with the one that is (and that's two, as is immediately established, therefore many), has to do with particulars, with things.

All the hypotheses examine their assumptions and definitions about the one in terms of a series of attributes or what Plato calls "contrary characters" (tanantia). The list is nearly the same in all cases, although the later hypotheses make short shrift of it. In the first hypothesis, the One has none of them, while in the second it has all of them. This is not hard for us to understand, given what we now already know, at least for the first five in each, because these are bodily or spatial characteristics, which obviously abstractions do not have, but particular things do have. The next five (omitting one bodily character in the second hypothesis, touch, which seems strangely out of place there) have to do with relations. Their status is more problematical. The arguments about these are more difficult, and appear more sophistical, but most of them make use of the ambiguity of Form and particular to effect their conclusions. One of the reasons that the second hypothesis is so much longer than the first is that it seems to take more argument to show that the one possesses both of two contrary characters, than to show that it has neither. Another reason is the problems encountered with the presence of time.

As the charts above show, the remaining hypotheses also pair up to deal with the one in its abstract and in its particular states.

Hypothesis 3 assumes that the others somehow participate in unity (157C1). This is indeed true of other things. They are a multitude of individual things. They also have all the attributes. They are, of course, other than a particular one.

Hypothesis 4 assumes (159B6-C4) that the Others and the One are utterly separate from each other. These are Forms.

Hypothesis 5, especially at 162A1-B3, shows us Plato's Parmenides taking issue directly with the real Parmenides' famous dicta in DK VII, 1 and DK II, 3. Ou gar mEpote touto damEi einai mE eonta and ouk esti mE einai forbid us to say that not-being is. How does this come about? It all depends upon which you are talking about, absolutes or particulars.

The last four hypotheses repeat the pattern of the first four, but for the one that is not, and with some other differences. The situation is tricky. The One of hypothesis 5 has all the contrary characters. Extrapolating our experience in the first four, we would expect it to be a particular one. Not at all. It is a particular one that is *not*, but that leaves the One as a Form that is. The presence of the negative has reversed the field. The fact that there is knowledge of it confirms this: it is conceptual, not perceptual knowledge. So does the admission (160B7-8) that the one that is not differs from the not-one that is not. Furthermore its participation in Others is participation in other Ideas, after the manner of the *Sophist*, 253B-259B. So this one that is not, in hypothesis 5, is a copy, but the One that is is a Form.

Absolute Not-being is distinguished at 160C4 from particular not-being, which is otherness. Thus is broached the question of the two states of negation, to parallel the two states of unity and being, broached in the first and second hypotheses. The two states and the reversal of their application are summed up at 160E7: einai men dE tOi heni ouk hoion te, eiper ge mE esti, metechein de pollOn ouden kOluei, alla kai anagkE…The negative absolute possesses characteristics of the positive particular.

Hypothesis 6 deals with the One that is not in any way whatsoever: oudamOs oudamE estin oude pEi metechei ousias to ge mE on (163C6-7). This one is not even a Form, much less a copy, and of course, not existing in any way whatsoever, neither can there be any contrary characters. Thus the sixth denies what the fifth affirms, and it is to this state of not-being that the real Parmenides' strictures, noted just above, truly apply.

Hypothesis 7. With the last two hypotheses we have come to a double negative: if there is not a one, what happens to the others? The others are not the one that is not, in seven. If we are talking about particular things, this makes perfectly good sense: just because one is not, others need not be not. They may well be. Furthermore, the field being reversed again by the double negative, they have the contrary characters. Thus:

Hypothesis	Contrary Characters
1	no
2	yes
3	yes
4	no
5	yes
6	no
7	yes
8	no

The 8th hypothesis parallels the sixth. It is again the Form of the One that is not; otherwise, as in the seventh, there would be others—and there are not, neither one nor many (165E4-8). And since there are no others, there can be no Others. Others would be other in such a case. And there are no contrary characters. There is nothing at all.

Taken all together the eight hypotheses exhibit various symmetries of structure. Three have been exhibited. Here is a fourth. One may tabulate their relationships with each other, according to their subjects and assumptions, as follows:

	A Form/copy	B one/other	C being/not-being
1	2	4	6
2	1	3	5
3	4	2	7
4	3	1	8
5	6	7	2
6	5	8	1
7	8	5	3
8	7	6	4

This table of pairings is helpful in discovering and keeping in mind what Plato is saying, and it exhibits again how highly structured is the main part of the dialogue.

CONTEXT

What is the point of all this? Do you think that it is just a game or a puzzle or an exercise? For one thing, it deals with problems, being and not-being, unity and multiplicity, that had bothered the ancient Greeks for a long time. For another, it deals with central doctrines of both Parmenides and Plato: being and the Forms. We can see here that Plato recognized what few if any others recognized: Parmenides' One Being of DK VIII, 5—6, etc., epei nun estin homou pan, hen, suneches, etc., was not an immobile, undifferentiated universe, a notion that no one could rightly put up with, but it was an abstraction as we would call it, a Form! Dimly recognized, perhaps, but nevertheless just that: the Form of Being. Plato surpassed Parmenides by recognizing that there were other abstractions, other Forms, too. But Parmenides' estin was in fact the first, even though not named as such by him.

We have seen above how the *Parmenides*, 162A1-B3, addresses directly the problem of not-being raised by Parmenides in DK VII, 1 and DK II, 3. Plato had dealt with this after one fashion in the *Sophist*. We can see now that the solution there was based upon the ambiguity of negation: not-being and otherness. Here in the fifth and sixth hypotheses he argues from the ambiguity of Form v. copy, abstract v. particular. As a Form (abstraction) Not-being is, but as a particular it is not. There is no question that Plato in the *Parmenides* has the real Parmenides very much in mind.

His own Form theory is also part of the context for these eight hypotheses. A number of the problems and paradoxes that attend the theory are raised here. What sort of being does the Form of the One have? In the first hypothesis it does not exist. In the fifth, if there is not a one, the Form of the One somehow is. In the fourth hypothesis the Form of the Others has no unity, certainly an aberration in Plato's theory as we know it otherwise.

Not only did the *Parmenides* have a context in the traditions of its time, but it also provided a possible context for later times that was ignored, probably because it was not even understood. I do not refer to the stimulus it provided for the great neoplatonic tradition. That was something else. But it embodies a way of thinking in terms of paradox, a logic, that was completely lost from sight. Aristotelian and Stoic logic became the Greek legacy to the following ages. The fundamental rule of thought was and still is Aristotle's famous law of contradiction (*Metaphysics*, Gamma, iii—vii). The rule of Plato's *Parmenides* is: the same *can* belong and not belong to the same subject, the same *can* be and not be, opposites *can* be attributed to the same at the same time, contradicting Aristotle's three formulations of the law, omitting only "in the same respect", kata to auto. But that is precisely the point. There is no same respect where Form and copy, abstract and concrete, mind and body are involved, and these are basic suppositions of the human condition. We will return to this point later.

THE STRUCTURE OF THE DIALOGUE AS A WHOLE

The dialogue as a whole is divided into two parts, an introductory part and a main part. The introductory part creates the setting and relates a conversation between Zeno, Socrates and Parmenides. This leads easily to the main part, which is a demonstration by Parmenides. Here is briefest statement of the structure of the whole dialogue:

I. Introduction   126A1-137C3

  A. The setting and characters   126A1-127D5

  B. Conversation between Zeno and Socrates   127D6-130A2
    1. Zeno's hypothesis: if things are many...
    2. Socrates' reply: the theory of Forms

  C. Parmenides' critique of Socrates'   130A3-136C5
    theory and of Zeno's method

  D. Proposal for a demonstration by Parmenides   136C6-137C3

II. Parmenides' demonstration: eight hypotheses   137C4-166C5
about the one

  A. If there is a one,
    1. what must we say about it?
      (two hypotheses)
    2. what must we say about the others?
      (two hypotheses)

B. If there is not a one,
    1. what must we say about it?
       (two hypotheses)
    2. what must we say about the others?
       (two hypotheses)

The second part (II) is the *raison d'être* of the whole, and the part which usually causes the most amazement and difficulty. But let us first take a closer look at the first and introductory part. This may be outlined in greater detail as follows.

THE INTRODUCTORY PART, 126A1-137C3

THE STRUCTURE OF THE INTRODUCTORY PART

A. The setting and the persons	126A1-127D5
B. Conversation between Zeno and Socrates	127D6-130A2
1. Zeno's hypothesis: if things are many, they are both like and unlike, which is impossible, etc.	D6-E5
2. Socrates' reply	E6-130A2
a. preliminary exchange between Socrates and Zeno	E6-128E4
b. Socrates' critique of Zeno's hypothesis: the theory of Forms; things can participate in opposite Forms. See esp. 129B1-C1.	128E5-130A2
C. Parmenides' critique of Socrates' theory and of Zeno's method	130A3-136C5
1. seven problems raised by Socrates' theory	A3-134E8
a. the extent of the Forms	A3-E4
b. is the whole of the Form in the participant?	E4-131C11
c. is a part?	C12-E7
d. infinite regress (first mode)	E8-132B6
e. are Forms just thoughts?	B7-C11

19

THE CONVERSATION BETWEEN ZENO AND SOCRATES: THE THEORY OF FORMS (127D6-130A2)

That outline indicates how easily and naturally the conversation led up to the climax at the end of the introductory part, wherein Parmenides was persuaded to undertake the demonstration that comprises the whole of the main part of the dialogue. Zeno's hypothesis led to Socrates' rebuttal, which led in turn to Parmenides' rejoinder to them both, explicitly to Socrates, implicitly to Zeno in his plan for training. This in turn led to the entreaty to Parmenides to demonstrate what he meant. But there is more than art at stake here. Several of the terms are introduced in this conversation which will figure in the later demonstration: the One and the Many of course (established Eleatic themes), also likeness and unlikeness, whole and part, and the Equal, the Large and the Small. All these will be explicitly mentioned in the main part. There are others that are not so explicitly mentioned later, but nevertheless play a part: above all the theory of Forms.

Although Zeno's hypothesis initiates the conversation, there can be little doubt that the theory of Forms, which we know of course as Plato's theory, is the main theme of the introduction (126A1-137C3). Socrates' exposition of it, and Parmenides' critique and ultimate partial approval (135E5-C3) of it, form the larger share of this part. The significance of this will become apparent in the eight hypotheses, where it plays a major role.

One must always keep in mind the historical background, so far as we know it, of this conversation and of the main figures in it. The conversation is part fiction, part fact. It is fiction with a factual background. Such a conversation never did take place, and some of the views of the speakers are not their views as we know these from other sources. But some of the views *are* views that we know from other sources that they held, and yet other views seem to be fairly drawn implications of views that they did hold. Here we are on the borderline between fact and fiction.

For example, the theory of Forms is generally accepted without question as Plato's invention, not Socrates' as this dialogue would have us believe. But Plato himself in his early and (it is widely believed) more historical dialogues (e.g., *Euthyphro*, 5D, 6D; *Phaedo*, 65D, 74A-B, 100B-D) seems to indicate that the germ of the idea came from Socrates. Aristotle confirms this in *Metaphysics*, 987b1-11, 1078b17-34.

The Form theory which Socrates raises in the dialogue as a criticism of Zeno is *really* being raised by Plato as an explanation of the real Parmenides. Parmenides had in fact become notorious for the problem he had raised in his philosophical poem, perhaps a hundred years or so before this dialogue was written:

...epei nun estin homou pan,

hen, suneches,...　　　　　　　(DK VIII, 5—6)

Everything is one! This statement we accept as a historical fact. It is also a fact that all his contemporaries and successors (so far as we know) understood that Parmenides was making the absurd and impossible suggestion that the whole universe is one single, immovable, impartible unity. There could be no plurality or change. Hence Zeno's supporting hypothesis with which this dialogue commences. It was the famous Eleatic thesis that he was supporting. But this dialogue may be evidence that Plato saw through this, and in his eyes there was a sense in which Parmenides was quite right and not the least bit absurd. This sense is supplied by the theory of Forms, as we shall in due course see. The theory of Forms plays a major role throughout the whole of the second and main part, Parmenides' demonstration. It can also be seen to have played a part, however unconscious he may have been of the fact, in the real Parmenides' real statement about the unity of being. If Being was a Form, he was right.

PARMENIDES' CRITIQUE OF THE THEORY OF FORMS, 130A3-135E7

The critique of the theory of Forms, which Plato puts into the mouth of Parmenides, in the introductory part, deserves closer inspection. The text appears to contain seven problems, which may be outlined as follows:

a. the extent of the Forms   130A3-E4

    1 One and Many?   B5
    2 Beautiful and Good?   B8
    3 Man?   C1
    4 Hair, and Mud and Dirt?   C6
    5 Socrates' hesitant response   D3-9
    6 Parmenides' fatherly advice   E1-4

b. is the whole of the Form in the participant?   E4-131C11

    1 Parmenides explains the difficulty   E4-131B2
    2 Socrates' rebuttal; non-material   B3-6
       analogy of "day", ignored by Parmenides
    3 Parmenides' analogy of "sail";   B7-C11
       Socrates agrees that the Form is a part

1 Forms are unknowable to us　　　　　　　　　　A11-134C3
　　a difficulty convincing the agnostic　　　　　A11-C2
　　b Forms are not in us (or in our　　　　　　C3-7
　　　　world, en hEmin); they are by themselves
　　c Forms of relation are related to　　　　　C8-D6
　　　　themselves, not to our world, and vice-versa
　　d examples:
　　　　(1) masters & slaves v. absolute　　　　　D7-134A2
　　　　　　mastery and absolute slavery
　　　　(2) absolute knowledge is of absolute truth　A3-5
　　　　(3) and each kind of absolute knowledge is　A6-8
　　　　　　of each kind of absolute truth
　　　　(4) our knowledge is of our truth,　　　　A9-B2
　　　　　　and each of our kinds of knowledge
　　　　　　is of each of our kinds of things
　　e recall of major premiss: the Forms　　　　B3-5
　　　　are not in us (refers to 133C5)
　　f each absolute class is known by　　　　　B6-8
　　　　its own kind of knowledge
　　g we don't know them or any of the Forms　　B9-C3
2 God has no knowledge of or relation to us　　C4-E8
　　a absolute knowledge is more accurate　　　C4-9
　　　　and better than our knowledge
　　b no one has better title to this than God　C10-12
　　c God cannot have knowledge of us　　　　D1-8
　　d concluding summary　　　　　　　　　D9-E8

This is a fairly straightforward outline of Parmenides' critique just as Plato gives it, aimed first of all to assist us in following the text. It does not however emphasize the key points or elicit the significant implications. To these ends, one might reorganize the outline along the following lines.

The first problem, or question, a., is in effect postponed. The next two, b. and c., are really two parts of one question, and they include an important suggestion by Socrates, i.e., his non-material analogy ("day") that is ignored by Parmenides. It will come up again shortly, only slightly altered.

The third part of this critique comprises the two arguments based upon infinite regress. The second one, f., is really only a revision of the first, d., brought about by an intervening incident, e. In e., Socrates again suggests that the Forms are non-material: they are thoughts, he says, and are only in our minds. Parmenides replies with a question that seems unanswerable (132C9-11), and Socrates drops it and passes on to another suggestion, the one that leads to the second infinite regress argument, f.

That it seems unsatisfactory here, does not mean that Socrates' suggestion is a bad one. On the one hand it raises a question that, although unanswerable, has remained with us for nearly twenty four hundred years, and is still with us today. It was the universals question of the twelfth century and is the mind-body question of our time (Are thoughts things, e.g. neurons? Are things thoughts? What is the relation between things and thoughts?). On the other hand, it is the question that the present critique by Parmenides returns to in its last part, g.: Parmenides' question about the relation of the Forms to us.

Plato himself calls this the "greatest" problem (133B4). What is it? The text in its simplicity of language is not easy to interpret here. The basis of the argument is that the Forms are not en hEmin. What does this mean? 'In us'? "In our world"? Later he uses also the words, par hEmin (133C9-10, 134B4). He also uses the verb, echomen (134B3): we do not "have" hem. He probably does not mean here "in us" in the sense of "in our minds". He has already had his Socrates make the suggestion and his Parmenides reject it. Plato did not think of the Ideas as just in the mind, even though later generations did. It was not his way. He seems to mean here something more like "in our world" (as Cornford indeed translates here). The purport of this whole section, g., is the contrast between the world of Forms and our world, the world of bodies. The world of Ideas may not *be* only in the mind, to Plato, but still it is approachable only with the mind, and again, although he does not put the world of Ideas in the mind, he most emphatically severs it from our bodily world. He took the first step; others took the second. And even if he failed to take the second, he implied it explicitly here in Socrates' key suggestion in the very middle of this critique: aren't these Forms thoughts, in our minds (133B3-5)? So this critique by Parmenides of Socrates' theory of Forms discloses to our inspection the gradual development of this profound problem: what or where are the Forms? 1. Are they material or non-material (ignored)? 2. Are they thoughts, in the mind (not really answered, but only turned into another question)? 3. How can there be any relation between the Forms in one "world" and us in another? How can we know anything about them? In short, Parmenides' critique does not deny the existence of Forms. Far from it. The critique is concluded by his avowal to Socrates that we must believe in them in any case (135B5-C4). They exist, and are apprehended with the mind. It simply raises questions that we are still struggling to answer. What are these Ideas that we apprehend with the mind, and how are they related to our bodily world and selves? Whatever they are, we will find that the main part of the dialogue is organized with them in view.

THE SUMMARY AND EXHORTATION TO SOCRATES, 134E9-135E7

The important thing to note about this section is that Plato goes to some length to show that Parmenides has far from rejected Socrates' arguments out of hand, nor thinks that he has proven Socrates wrong. The question has not been resolved. It remains an aporia, which Socrates is encouraged to prepare himself carefully to pursue. Of course we must keep reminding ourselves that what we have here in this dialogue between Parmenides and Socrates (and others) is really Plato talking with himself, and perhaps also to us. In any case, the Forms, the Ideas, these abstractions remain to be explained. It is a brief exchange, 135B5-C4, that throws everything in question again.

PARMENIDES' PLAN FOR TRAINING, 135E8-136C5

The plan which Parmenides now outlines briefly (136A5-B1) is precisely the scheme which he himself follows in the second or main part of the dialogue (137C4-166C5), substituting there the one for the many as the subject of the inquiry. He says here:

> "If there is a many, what must we say about them (or attribute to them, ti chrE sumbainein), with regard to themselves and with regard to the one, and about the one, with regard to itself and with regard to the many; and again, if there is *not* a many. what are we to say about the one and the many with regard to themselves and to each other (136A5-B1)."

Compare this with the scheme of Parmenides' own inquiry which follows in the main part of the dialogue:

If there is a one, what are we to say about

the one itself?	1
the one in relation to the others?	2
the others in relation to the one?	3
the others themselves?	4

If there is not a one,

he one itself?	5
he one in relation to the others?	6
he others in relation to the one?	7
he others themselves?	8

Aside from reversing the inquiry, commencing from the standpoint of the one instead of that of many, the only other substantive difference is the substitution of the others (talla) for the many (ta polla).

THE PROPOSAL FOR A DEMONSTRATION
AND ENTREATY TO PARMENIDES

This section, 136C6-137C3, concludes the first part, and fluently and naturally introduces the second or main part of the dialogue. We might easily overlook the reference to Ibycus and his horse here (136E9-137A4) as merely another piece of rhetoric on Plato's part. However, it is especially significant in revealing Parmenides' state of mind. The easiest place to take the measure of Ibycus, after the brief articles in the *Oxford Classical Dictionary* and *Der Kleine Pauly*, is in the second volume of the Loeb Classical Library edition of *Lyra Graeca*, p. 78-87. Beside being a poet of note in the sixth century, he seems to have had a reputation of being what we would call today a "great lover." gegone de erOtomanestatos peri meirakia (Suidas), "he was mad with love for young lads." Apparently he just couldn't quit, as he got older, even though it was getting a bit difficult for him. Thence his lines about the old race horse, and quite apt they are. Parmenides, likening himself to Ibycus and his horse, reveals the intensity of his love for dialectic, his inability to refrain, and the difficulty of performing the task that he is faced with in the main part of the dialogue.

MAIN PART: THE DEMONSTRATION BY PARMENIDES (137C4-166C5)

PRELIMINARY OBSERVATIONS

Plato has introduced the main part of his dialogue, and given us a hint about its structure, but before proceeding further these observations are in order:

1. First of all, there has been disagreement about the number of hypotheses that Parmenides considers. The neoplatonists counted nine. This view began perhaps with Plotinus (*Ennead* V, 1, 8, lines 24-27) and is most evident in Proclus (for a fuller account see H. D. Saffrey and L. G. Westerink, ed., *Proclus, Théologie Platonicienne, Livre I*, Paris, 1968, esp. chap. I, sect. 7). It was peculiar and appropriate to the neoplatonist theology.

F. M. Cornford adopted a middle course. In his arrangement there are eight hypotheses *and* a corollary, hypotheses 2a. The corollary is Proclus' third hypothesis.

In our outline there are eight hypotheses. The neoplatonists' third, and Cornford's corollary, are part of the second hypothesis in our scheme, nothing more. This leaves us with the task of explaining a textual peculiarity at 155E4-5, and this will be done when we come to it. Meanwhile, a justification of eight hypotheses has already been suggested by Parmenides' own words above (135E8-136C5). Such a structure conforms to his stated intention. In addition the symmetry of the eight is a strong argument in their favor.

2. Secondly, the internal structure of the hypotheses will be easier to understand if we anticipate a special feature to be found in them.

Parmenides develops and tests (so to speak) each of his hypotheses with a peculiar set of terms, a fixed list of contraries. Cornford called them "contrary characters," and we adopt that term here. Plato himself gave them a name, alluding to them several times in hypotheses 3 and 4 (157B1, 159A1 and 7, E5, 160A2). He called them ta enantia pathE or simply ta enantia (tanantia). Mostly he just uses them, pair by pair. They can be listed, thus:

whole	part
limited	unlimited
straight	curved
in itself	in another
at rest	in motion
same	other
like	unlike
equal	unequal
older	younger
in contact	not in contact

This list is unique to the *Parmenides*. Many of these pairs appear elsewhere, but not as part of just such a list. One is reminded of the list of ten pairs of contraries, the sustoichia, that Aristotle ascribed to the Pythagoreans (*Metaphysics*, A, 5, 986a23-26). Indeed, three of Plato's pairs appear on the Pythagorean list. Whatever its origin, it is this list of contrary characters that Parmenides uses in each of the hypotheses of the ensuing demonstration. We will meet them over and over again.

3. The arguments large and small are frequently framed around an ambiguity. The apparent contradictions that the one does and does not have the contrary characters (hypotheses 1 and 2) or that the one has both of a pair of contrary characters (hypothesis 2), for example, make use of ambiguities in our notions of one, or in our notions of the various contrary characters. It is these contradictions and by implication their underlying ambiguities that have elicited the varied responses to this dialogue, causing

some to see it as a game, others as a parody, yet others as an exercise, and so forth. Little wonder. They could be taken in any of these ways. If we are going to ask if there is a serious point to this demonstration of the *Parmenides*, it is precisely these ambiguities that we are going to have to identify and evaluate. We will be able to signal some of them, such as of the one and the others, by capitalizing the initial letters when it is clear that it is the Form that is meant, and by using lower case when it is clear that it is not. But even this is not always clear, and in some cases, when both or either are meant, the lower case will be used. The Greek text makes no such use of capitals, of course. It is only the purpose of the outline and commentary to help make these ambiguities clear.

4. One of the difficulties of this demonstration is the need to keep in mind at the same time several arguments that are going on at several structural levels. For example, if one is following a detailed argument in the middle of the second hypothesis, one has also to keep in mind the developing contrast with first. When one comes to the third and fourth hypotheses, one has their contrast with the first two to think about, as well as their contrast with each other; and in the last four, theirs with the first four, as well as their pairs with each other, and singly with each other. This is, needless to say, sometimes rather taxing. The outlines should help us to cope with these multiple demands.

5. We must be on our guard to distinguish between (1) terms used to refer to or deal with the subjects of the argument, and (2) terms used as subjects of the arguments themselves. The distinction is similar to the distinction that computer programmers make between (1) address arithmetic and (2) calculation. It is an especially vexatious problem here where so many of the terms that we will be talking about will be the same as the terms that we use to talk about them. To make up a brief and exaggerated example, consider the following statement: this demonstration deals with two topics; one is the other, and the other is the one. That statement contains two

words, each of which is used twice, one time as a term of address, the other, as a term of substance!

6. We must keep in mind that we will be dealing in this demonstration with two kinds of negatives. This ambiguity does not stand out quite so obviously as the other two ambiguities of one and being do. Abstraction and particularity of unity and being are evident in the pairings of 1 and 2, 3 and 4, 5 and 6, 7 and 8. The abstraction and particularity of negation are to be found in the comparison of 5, 6, 7 and 8 with 3, 4, 7 and 8. The last four hypotheses deal with the one that is not ("If there is not a one…"). The third, fourth, seventh and eighth deal with the others. They also are not one. In the last two hypotheses, in which we deal with both of these together (others than the one that is not), we will be dealing with double negatives. All of these ambiguities of unity, being and negation have tended to be obscured by the starker contrasts of being and not being, one and others that stands out in the pairings 1—4 v. 5—8 and 1, 2, 5, 6 v. 3, 4, 7, 8. When Parmenides first enunciated his plan (136A5-B1), he used the words pros hauta, pros allEla and so forth. He might as well have used kath' hauta, kath' allEla, etc. kath' hauta is one of Plato's customary ways of referring to abstractions. In any case, the subjects of hypotheses 1, 4, 6, and 8 are abstractions, the Form of the One, and the subjects of hypotheses 2, 3, 5 and 7 are particular ones. The conclusions follow a somewhat different pattern, but the ambiguity of Form and copy of unity, being and negation remain controlling.

Ambiguity, complexity, terms of address and substance, double negatives—all these are going to make the ensuing demonstration difficult to follow. Outlines will help.

OUTLINE OF THE HYPOTHESES AND THEIR ASSUMPTIONS

A. If there is a one,

1. the first hypothesis deals with the abstract One, i.e. One as a Form. It is only One. allo ti ouk an eiE polla to hen. It is neither other nor many. It is called hen hen at 142C3. It does not even exist.

2. the second hypothesis deals with particular ones. They participate in existence. hen ei estin, ara hoion te auto einai men, ousias de mE metechein;—ouk an hoion te (142B5-7). It is not only one. It is at least two, and therefore many.

3. the third hypothesis deals with particulars, one and others. The others somehow participate in unity. oude mEn steretai ge pantapasi tou henos talla, alla metechei pEi (157C1-2). This is indeed true of all the everyday things around us.

4. the fourth hypothesis deals with the Forms of the One and the Others. They are both utterly separate from each other. ar' oun ou chOris men to hen tOn allOn, chOris de talla tou henos einai;...nai...Oudeni ara tropOi metechoi an talla tou henos...(159B6-7, D1). Plato's vaunted unity of the Forms breaks down here, as did their existence in the first hypothesis.

B. If there is *not* a one,

5. the fifth hypothesis makes it clear that it is something quite distinct that is not, thus the one that is not somehow *is*. heteron ti leg[ei] to mE on (160C4)...einai men dE tOi heni ouk hoion te, eiper ge mE esti, metechein de pollOn ouden kOluei, alla kai anagkE (160E7-161A1)...kai mEn kai ousias ge dei auto metechein pEi (161E3). There is knowledge of it. This One that somehow is, is a Form. It is a copy that it is not.

6. the sixth hypothesis states that when we say that it is not, we don't mean anything else than to deny it all being. to de mE estin hotan legomen, ara mE ti allo sEmainei H ousias apousian toutOi hOi an

phOmen mE einai; ouden allo (163C2-3)...oudamOs
oudamEi estin oude pEi metechei ousias to ge mE on (163C6-7).
The one in no way whatsoever is. No way at all. Neither Form nor
copy. In the hypothesis here it is the Form that must be meant,
since, as we saw in the fifth, if it were a copy, such a conclusion
would not hold true. There might be a Form, and thus it might
somehow participate in being—which it does not, here. We conclude that in this hypothesis neither Form nor copy exist. houto dE
hen ouk on ouk echei pOs oudamei (164B3). There is not one
thing, nor any Idea.

7. the seventh hypothesis commences with the assertion that the others must be somehow, otherwise they could not be spoken of. alla
mEn pou dei auta einai, ei gar mEde estin, ouk an peri tOn allOn
legoito (164B6-7). The others here are both things and Form, and
the one is one thing. Clearly, if there is not one thing there are others. And if they can be spoken of, there is an Idea of them.

8. the eighth hypothesis states that, if there is not a One, the others
will not be one. oukoun hen men ouk estai talla (165E4). Nor
many. oude mEn polla ge, en gar pollois ousin eneiE an kai hen
(E5). The One that is not must be a Form. If it were a copy, there
would be others, as we saw in the seventh, above, and they would
be ones. The others that are neither one nor many (again, mE
enontos de henos en tois allois, oute polla oute hen esti talla,
165E7-8) are Form and copies. There is nothing: hen ei mE estin,
ouden estin (166C1).

THE INTERNAL STRUCTURE OF THE HYPOTHESES

Although the subjects and assumptions differ in each hypothesis, the
internal structure of each of them is the same or similar. Each examines its

subject in terms of ten pairs of contrary characters. The parallelism of their treatment is attenuated as the demonstration proceeds, but it remains to the end in some measure. For example, up to a point (g. in the following outline) the first two hypotheses follow the same arrangement. Thereafter some differences appear. And the first four hypotheses all start with the consideration whether their subjects are wholes with parts, while the last four start with the consideration of other characters. Also the later hypotheses tend to be briefer than the earlier ones. This internal symmetry of the hypotheses (and its attenuation) is evident in an outline, and such an outline will also be a useful guide as we proceed to examine the hypotheses individually and in greater detail.

OUTLINE OF THE HYPOTHESES AND THEIR ARGUMENTS

A. If there is a one, 137C4-160B4

   1. it has none of the contrary characters. C4-142A8
      The One is not other or many. allo ti
      ouk an eiE polla to hen (C4-5). The One
      is absolutely One, nothing else. It is
      hen hen (142C2).

     a. it has no parts, nor is a whole   C5-D3
     b. it has no beginning or end, is infinite   D4-8
     c. it has no shape, is not round or straight   D8-138A1
     d. it is nowhere, not in itself or another   A1-B6
     e. it cannot move or rest   B7-139B3
     f. it is not same or other, as (than)   B4-E6
       itself or others
     g. it is not like or unlike itself or others   E7-140B5
     h. not equal nor unequal to itself or others   B6-D8
     i. it is not nor becomes older or younger   E1-141D6
       or the same age, nor is it in time, nor

has anything to do with time

    j. it does not exist or participate in being   D7-142A8
       nor *is* one; there is no name, account or
       knowledge or perception or opinion of it.

2. it partakes of being: hen ei estin, ara hoion   142B1-157B5
   te auto einai men, ousias de mE metechein;
   —ouk hoion te (B5-7). Its being is not the
   same as its unity: oukoun kai hE ousia tou
   henos eiE an ou tauton ousa tOi heni...
   (B7-8). Again: esti de ou to auto hE te ousia
   kai to hen D2-3). This hypothesis is not
   ei hen hen, but ei hen estin (C2-3). It has
   all the contrary characters.

    a. it is a whole, with parts   C7-D9
    b. it is infinite and limited   D9-145A4
    c. it has shape, round or straight   A4-B5
    d. it is in itself and in another   B6-E6
    e. it moves and rests   E7-146A8
    f. it is the same and other as (than)   A9-147B8
       itself and others
    g. it is like and unlike itself and others   C1-148D4
    h. it touches and does not touch itself   D5-149 D7
       and others
    i. it is equal and unequal to itself and   D8-151E2
       others
    j. it does and does not partake of time,   E3-157B5
       be and become younger and older than
       itself and others.

3. the others are not one, but they do not   157B6-159B1
   wholly lack unity; they participate in it

somehow. oukoun eipeiper alla tou henos
estin, oute to hen esti talla…oude mEn
steretai ge pantapasi tou henos talla, alla
metechei pEi (157B8-C2). It is as particulars,
rather than abstractions, that they participate
in unity as well as plurality. They have all the
contrary characters.

   a. they have parts and are a whole C3-158B4
   b. they are infinite in number and limited B5-D8
   c. they are like and unlike E1-159A6
   d. they are subject to all the other A6-B1
      contrary characters

4. The Others and the One are utterly separate   159B2-160B4
   ar' oun ou chOris men to hen tOn allOn, chOris
   de talla tou henos einai;…nai (159B6-7)…
   oudeni ara tropOi metechoi an talla tou henos (D1).
   The Others, as the One, are a Form. They have
   none of the contrary characters.

a. they are not parts or wholes	C5-D3
b. they are not one or many	D3-E1
c. they are not like or unlike	E2-160A3
d. they have none of the other contrary characters	A4-B2
e. recap of the first four hypotheses	B2-4

B. If there is not a one,   160B5-166C2

5. it is something distinct, and there is   160B6-163B6
   knowledge of it, an idea (Idea) of it. dEloi
   hoti heteron ti to mE on (C4)…gnOston ti
   legei (C7-8). It is a Form, and it participates
   in many Ideas, metechein de pollOn ouden kOluei,

alla anagkE (E8-161A1). It has the contrary characters:

a. unlikeness and likeness	A6-C2
b. inequality, equality, greatness, smallness	C3-E2
c. being and not being	E3-162B8
d. it moves and rests	B9-E3
e. it changes and does not change	E4-163A7
f. it comes into being and passes away, and does not come into being nor pass away	A7-B6

6. it simply is not, and does not participate   163B7-164B4
in being in any way whatsoever, ara mE ti
allo sEmainei E ousias apousian toutOi Oi
an phOmen mE einai; ouden allo (163C2-4)…
oudamOs oudamE estin oude pEi metechei ousias
to ge mE on (C6-7). Neither Form nor copy,
it has none of the contrary characters.

a. it does not come into being or pass away	D1-8
b. it does not change, move or rest	D8-E6
c. it has no greatness, smallness, equality, likeness, difference, thisness, thatness, etc.	E6-164B1
d. there is no knowledge or opinion or perception or reasoning or name of it, or anything else	B1-2
e. recap: it is not, in any way whatsoever	B3-4

7. the others must *be* somehow, otherwise   164B5-165E1
one could not speak of them. alla mEn pou dei
auta einai, ei gar mEde alla estin, ouk an peri
tOn allOn legoito (B6-7). They must be as a Form,
since they can be spoken of, and if the one that
is not is a particular thing, then the others may
be particular things too. Surely, if there is not
one thing, there may be others. And they must be
other than others (B8-C8). In any case they have

the contrary characters.

a.	they appear unlimited and limited, one and many, etc.	C8-165C6
b.	they appear like and unlike	C6-D4
c.	same and other	D5
d.	in touch with each other and separate	D5-6
e.	moving and at rest	D6
f.	coming to be, passing away, and neither,	D7
g.	and all other such	D8-E1

8. the others are neither one nor many,   165E2-166C2
oukoun hen men ouk estai talla…
oude mEn polla ge (E4-5)…mE
eontos de henos en tois allois, oute
polla oute hen esti talla (E7-8). Nor do
they appear one or many, or have or appear
to have any of the contrary characters.

a.	they are neither like nor unlike	B3-4
b.	nor same nor different	B4-5
c.	nor in touch nor separate	B5
d.	nor anything else	B5-7
e.	there is nothing	B7-C2

C. Recap of the eight hypotheses   C2-5

It is not a waste of time to repeat these outlines and commentary with slightly different emphases or levels of detail. This dialogue is sufficiently complicated that repetition is a help in grasping its contents. Thus we will go through the hypotheses once more, examining their assumptions and arguments in still greater detail. This is especially important for the verification of the scheme.

THE FIRST HYPOTHESIS

The first hypothesis commences with a succinct statement of its assumption, albeit in the form of a question and response: ei hen estin, allo ti ouk an eiE polla to hen; pOs gar an; "If there is a One, it can't be other [or] many, can it? How could it be?" (137C4-5). This One is in our modern terms an abstraction, in Plato's terms a Form, although nothing more is made of it now but to go on with the argument. The argument has ten parts, as we have outlined above. They involve the ten pairs of contrary characters that have also been outlined above. There is however more to the organization than just that. These ten sections, upon closer inspection, may be divided into three groups.

1. The first five arguments (137C5-139B3) are developed on the premiss of the very first (137C5-D3), that this One has no parts and is not a whole. They all have to do with physical characters, and Forms have no physical characters. The infinity under consideration here is a case in point. There are several kinds of infinity, raising possibilities of ambiguity that are played upon later on, but here only one kind is meant: it is an infinity of spatial (physical) extension, such as results from having no beginning or end. These are parts. Beginning, end, shape, place, motion, rest, all these are physical. Being interrelated, if the One has no parts, it has none of them.

So the key to this group is the initial conclusion, that the One has no parts nor is a whole. That it has no parts is obvious, else it would be many. That it is not a whole depends upon the additional assumption or definition (as you will) that parts and wholes reciprocally entail each other. ouchi ou an meros mEden apEi holon eiE; panu ge (137C7-D1). It seems a valid assumption about the physical world, that parts and wholes entail each other. The one will have both or neither (parts and whole): both if it is a physical thing, neither if it is not. Here it has neither: it is a Form.

In the first five arguments, then, it is the Form of the One that is assumed, and it is from physical things that this Form is distinguished. Once this is done in the case of the parts, the rest seems to follow quite naturally.

2.The next four arguments (139B4-141D6) have to do with relatives. These arguments are also interrelated, and they are more complex in their organization. This makes them a bit more difficult to follow. The complexity is due in part to the fact that opposite relatives are taken up together, and both of these are referred both to the subject itself (the One) and to one another. This raises acute problems about the nature of relations: can they be considered *per se*, to or by themselves? Plato sometimes thought not (*Sophist*, 255D; *Parmenides*, 139C4-5, etc.; Aristotle, by the way, thought not; see *Metaphysics*, A, 9, 990b16; see also Asclepius, *In Metaph.*, ed. Hayduck, p. 76). If not, then how can there be Forms of relations?

The first of these four arguments has itself four parts. The One is not

a. other than itself	B5-6
b. same as another	B7-C3
c. other than another	C3-D1
d. same as itself	D1-E6

The first two (B5-C3) of these four parts seem self-evident to us. In them the One is identified with itself or distinguished from the other. These are conclusions that are comfortable, because they are true of things as well as Forms, and thus are easy for us to recognize. The third part (C3-D1) depends upon a peculiarity of otherness just referred to above: ou gar heni prosEkei heterOi tinos einai, alla monOi heterOi heterou (139C4-5). Only an other can be other than another. Since the One is not other, it follows that it cannot be other than another. If it were not a Form, it could be other than another. The fourth part (D1-E6) is also based upon the supposition that the One is an utterly separate Form. Sameness would compromise this. Recapitulating, the first two parts of this argument (B5-C3) state consequences that apply equally to Forms and things, whereas the last two (C3-E6), to Forms only. Although these are negative consequences, the acute problem mentioned above is present, if partially concealed. It should be clear by now that in such a series of arguments which have the appearance of verbal trickery, it is not mere trickery at all. The arguments are based upon the distinction of things and Forms, and upon the peculiar natures of each, and upon the ambiguities that result. This will continue to be the case throughout the remainder of the dialogue.

The second of the four arguments of this group is that the One is not like or unlike itself or another (139E7-140B5). This is fairly simple and straightforward. It reiterates the prior argument, and adds the stipulation that likeness involves sameness, and unlikeness, otherness. It has two parts: the first (139E7-140A6) concludes that it is not like another or itself; the second (A6-B5), that it is not unlike itself or another.

The third of the four arguments (it is not equal or unequal to itself or another) has three parts, following its announcement in 140B6-7. The first part (140B7-C4) is a series of definitions of equal and unequal, unequal being represented by greater and smaller. The definition of equal (tOn autOn metrOn, B7-8) is simple. The definition of greater and smaller (= unequal) is somewhat more complex: they have either more or less of the same measures (C1-2), or, if it is their measures that are not the same (in size), it is greater than another of smaller measures and smaller than another of greater measures (C2-4). These last lines are severely elliptical. The second part (C4-8) eliminates equality to itself or another: it would participate in sameness. The third part (C8-D4) eliminates inequality in the guise of greater and smaller. It does so in two steps. First (C8-D1), this third part eliminates greater or smaller on account of having more or less of whatever measures, because measures are parts (tosautOn kai merOn an eiE, C9). Then, secondly (D2-4), it eliminates them in the case where the One itself is the measure (ei de ge henos metrou eiE..., D2): the argument from parts will not do in this case, but it would be equal and same. D4-8 is a recapitulation. The third argument looks to the first arguments in both this group and the prior group for its premisses.

The fourth and last of these four arguments of the middle group has two main parts. The first part (140E1-141A4) is devoted to showing that the One *is* not older or younger or the same age as itself or another, and has for its premisses the prior arguments about equality and inequality, likeness and unlikeness. The second (141A5-D6) is devoted to showing that the One does not *become* older or younger than itself, or the same age, since if it did it would be in time and partake of time, which it does not. It depends (141A5-6) on the immediately preceding part (140E1-141A4). In the distinction of *becoming* from *being* older, younger, etc., there is an ambiguity about time used here: time can mean a fixed or a growing continuum, a period (or instant) or a procession. This distinction is used here in passing from being to becoming, and again when it is argued that something in time is always becoming older and younger (141A6-B3) *and* always the same age (C4-7). In the first case it is the procession of time that is meant; in the second, the period or instant. This ambiguity will be used again in later hypotheses. Lines 141B3, pOs legeis;…C4, eoiken, seem almost a superfluous explanation.

In this group of four arguments, all are derived from the first, that the One is not the same or other than itself or another, excepting one case, in which inequality is eliminated on account of its having more or less measures, i.e. parts. And the first of this group, like the first of the prior group, is derived from the original supposition that this is the Form of the One which we have under scrutiny here, the utterly separate and abstract One alone, supposed in the beginning, which cannot be a whole or a part or same or other, because it cannot be other or many: allo ti ouk an eiE polla to hen (137C4-5).

. The last of the ten arguments of the first hypothesis (141D7-142A8) denies it being. This argument is ostensibly based upon the preceding argument, that the One does not participate in time, etc., and upon the contention that being is in time. However, that preceding argument is ultimately derived, as we just saw, from the original supposition that the One is an utterly abstract Form. This, its utter aloneness, is the real reason that the One cannot be, and you could argue directly from this reason to this result, with no intermediaries. The intermediate argument may be deceiving, taking our attention away from the real reason. The final argument then could have been the initial argument, with all else following. In fact one could also criticize the original statement, ei hen estin, allo ti ouk an eiH polla to hen (137C4-5) as self-contradictory. Plato's Parmenides himself implies this near the beginning of the next hypothesis (142C2): nun de ouch hautE estin hE hupothesis, ei hen hen, ti chrE sumbainein , all' ei hen estin. But do not let the semantic problem (how do we speak of this One Form, of the abstract One?) obscure the underlying problem: contradictory modes of being, i.e. Forms (abstractions, concepts, Ideas, ideas) v. things. These are what this hypothesis, this dialogue, and ultimately the whole of Plato's and Greek metaphysics and the modern mind-body controversies are primarily about.

Finally we can compare this hypothesis with its complementary hypotheses: if there is a One (Form), it is not (#1), but

1. (being) if there *is not* a One, there
   is not a one either (#6),
2. (negation) if there is a One, the
   Others (Form) is not in any way one (#4),
3. (unity) if there is one (copy), it is many (#2).

THE SECOND HYPOTHESIS

The second hypothesis is the longest by far of all the eight. In its structure it parallels the first very closely. The first eight arguments in both (a.—g.) deal with the same topics. The second hypothesis adds a new topic in the ninth argument (h.) that is not found in the first hypothesis: touch, hap-testhai. It appears to omit reference to the tenth or final topic of the first (existence and its concomitants) but really this occurs at the very begin-ning of the second, as we saw that it should or could in the first. The chief difference between the two hypotheses, which may account for the greater length of the second, is that the second attributes to the one all the char-acters that the first denies. Since these are contrary characters in all instances, they require lengthier explanations. The attribution of contrary characters will involve some fancy dialectic, and the use of a number of distinctions that have not been needed so far.

Having called attention to the tripartite division of the contrary characters in the first hypothesis, we will ignore that feature here, and take them up one by one. It may make the study of this long hypothesis a bit easier. But first of all there is the assumption to consider. hen ei estin, ara hoion te auto einai men, ousias de mE metechein; ouk hoion te (B5-7). This is the opposite of the assumption of the first hypothesis. So much is immedi-ately evident. The one, instead of being so utterly abstract that it cannot even be, here must partake of being, if it is. In case there might be any mistaking this, the difference is restated in the ensuing lines, B7-C7. Seldom in this dialogue is Plato as emphatic and unequivocal as he is in these lines. Everything that follows issues from this difference and from the plurality of the one being, which also mark it as not the Absolute One, but one thing.

1. First of all it has parts: one and being, C7-D5. It is also a whole (D6-9). Thus we see right away that things are both one and many, as opposed to the Absolute One or Form of the One, which is utterly separate and alone. The one thing can be a collection (of parts in a whole) or an individual part *or* whole), many or one, and other such ambiguities. Parts and wholes are one and many. They too are ambiguous. This section is so closely knit in the text with the assumption above, that it barely escapes

being confused with it. In the first hypthesis it was the *last* section (j.) that seemed thus close to the assumption of that hypothesis.

b. It is infinite and limited (142D9-145A4). Each of the parts has parts, since each part is and is one. This division may be carried on endlessly, like an infinite regress, the parts always possessing being and unity (142D9-143A3). Thus begins the second argument of this hypothesis. But there is much more to it than just that. It corresponds to 137D4-8 of the first hypothesis, but it is much longer and more complex. There the One was simply infinite, for negative reasons, with an infinity of extension: it had no beginning or end. Here the existent one is infinite in division and extension (by multiplication), and it is infinite both non-numerically and numerically. Then it is also limited. The argument runs to ninety two of Stephanus' lines, as opposed to five in the first hypothesis, and it begins and ends in the midst of his paragraphs. Here is an outline of the major headings of the argument:

1	the parts have parts, *ad infinitum* (infinity of division, without recourse to numbers)	142D9-143A3
2	infinity of multiplication, numerical	A4-144A9
3	infinity of division, parallel with existents	B1-E7
4	it is limited	E8-145A2
5	recap	A2

Section *1* gives little difficulty. It simply carries out the logic of the prior argument so faithfully that at first sight it may strike the reader as a part of that argument rather than the beginning of a new one.

Section *2* (A4-144A9) is deceptive. At first it may appear to the reader to be a digression that resuscitates the abstract One of the first hypothesis, and that mixes the two hypotheses, auto to hen, ho dE phamen ousias metechein (A6-7). Plato's absolute Ideas or Forms (auto...kath' hauto, 143A7) were never for him only in the mind (tEi dianoiai monon, *ibid*). But this turns out to be another argument for the infinity of the one, in endless number, an infinite multitude of beings. In Plato's system numbers are not Ideas or things, but something in between, ta metaxu (Aristotle, *Metaphysics*, passim, see Bonitz, *Index,* p. 461). Here he is concerned first of all to distinguish them from the existents (things) which he has just been talking about. The structure of section *2* is as follows:

a	distinction of the existent and conceptual ones	143A4-8
b	is the latter one or many?	A8-9
	(1) it is different from being, and difference is other than oneness	B1-8
	(2) one and difference, etc., are two, and, by extension, infinite number	C1-144A9
	(a) they are both	C1-9
	(b) both = 2	D1-2
	(c) both + each = 3	D2-7
	(d) 3 is odd; 2, even	D7-8
	(e) 2 is double; 3, triple	D8-E2
	(f) 2x2, 3x3, 3x2, 2x3, etc.	E3-7
	(g) even x odd, odd x even, etc.	E7-144A2
	(h) this leads to endless number	A2-5
	(i) as well as to an infinite multitude of beings	A5-9

At the conclusion of the argument (144A5-9) numbers are associated with being, pas arithmos ousias metechei (A7), in contrast to the situation at the beginning.

Perhaps the most important aspects of the argument are the insights it gives us into Plato's realistic view of Forms and his compromising view of numbers (metaxu). Forms are not mere figments of the mind (en tEi dianoiai monon, 143A7). The difference of one and its being, effected in the mind by our mental analysis, is different from the difference of Form and copy, and it requires the separate treatment given it here in this argument. This treatment by mental analysis makes use of numbers with their peculiar intermediate status. Plato's ontology is still imperfect in some respects.

Section 3 (144B1-E7) runs as follows:

a	the cutting up of existence into an infinite number of parts	B1-C2
b	and of the one into as many	C2-D5
c	goes hand in hand, is equal and infinite	D5-E5
d	recap	E5—7

The assumption that oneness parallels existence seems appropriate to the second hypothesis. The assumption that beings are infinitely divisible may be unobjectionable to us, but some of Plato's contemporaries might not have found it so. The transition preceding this section, A5-9, might be assigned to this section rather than the preceding one.

Section 4 (144E8-145A2) is a brief argument for the limitedness of the existent one, based upon the premisses of *a* parts being parts of wholes, and *b* wholes being limits. The first of these two premisses, the minor, kai mEn hoti ge holou ta moria moria (E8), is the same as the one used at the beginning of the first hypothesis, to meros pou holou meros estin (137C6). The second refers only to limit or infinity of extension, spatial or otherwise.

Section 5 recapitulates the assumption and the first two consequences of the second hypothesis, that is up to this point.

c. It has shape (A4-B5). The premiss is the preceding argument, or that last part of it which demonstrated that the existent one is limited. In this argument limit is now taken in its spatially extended sense.

d. It is in itself and in another (145B6-E6). This argument exhibits the following structure:

1	it is in itself: the one *qua* parts is in the one *qua* whole	B6-C7
2	the one *qua* whole is in another	C7-E3
a	it is not in its parts (i.e. wholly in, or in *qua* whole)	C7-8
	(1) it is not in all, because it is not in any one part (wholly)	D1-4
	(2) it is not in some, because the larger would be in the smaller	D5-7
b	if not in its parts, one, many or all	D7-E3
	(1) it must be in another	D8
	(2) if it were nowhere, it would be nothing	E1-2
3	recap	E3-6

Here is the other ambiguity of the one, related to the ambiguity of the collection and the individual: it can be a whole or a part. In section *2* there is a distinct meaning assumed for being "in its parts" (in = wholly in) which reflects this ambiguity. Note that there are other ways to argue that the existent one is *and is not* in itself and in another, if one is to use such ambiguities. The greatest one of all, i.e. to pan, the universe, is in itself and not in another, while all lesser ones are in another and not in themselves, if identity is not place (this was addressed by Aristotle in *Physics*, IV, iii—). This argument also leans on the ambiguity that the existent one is a whole or a part (a.).

e. It moves and rests. It stays put in relation to itself, but moves *qua* in another. The meaning of "in another" has changed from a static meaning (in the prior argument) to a moving one (in this). This argument has the immediately preceding one for its basis. It is the last of several arguments devoted for the most part to physical properties of the existent one, as in the first hypothesis. As in the first also, these arguments have for the most part their basis in the first of the series, that the existent one is a whole with parts. The exception is the argument for a numerical infinity of multiplication (143A4-144A9).

f. It is the same and other than itself and others (146A9-147B8). This argument has four parts, followed by the usual brief recapitulation: it is

1 same as itself	B2-C4
2 other than itself	C4-D1
3 other than others	D1-5
4 same as others	D5-147B6
5 recap	B6-8

Section *1* gives little difficulty. One thing is the same as itself, in the sense of identity or individuality, one of several possible senses of the one. The one as a part or a whole is ruled out (146B3-7) explicitly since these involve a collective sense of the one (collection of parts). If the statement that the one is not different from itself, oud' ara heautou ge heteron an eiE (C1-2), is plainly contradicted by the next section, that is because a different definition is assumed there.

Section *2*, other than itself (C4-D1), refers to the conclusions of the second prior argument (d., it is in itself and in another, 145B6-E6), which in turn depends upon definitions of the one as a whole and a part.

Section *3*, other than others (D1-5) tersely treats the argument as self evident. The same assumptions seem implied as in the first section. Compare 139C4-5 contradicting.

Section *4*, same as others (146D5-147B6), must obviously sieze upon the ambiguities of these terms. Let us outline this section, in an effort to detect them, as follows:

a	the one and the others are not different	D5-147A3
	(1) the Same and the Other are opposite to each other, auto te tauton kai to heteron enantia allElois	D5-D8
	(2) there is no other in any ***thing***, since it would be in a same thing (anything that endures in time is the same), ouden esti tOn ontOn En hO…, etc.	D9-E4
	(3) whether one or not-one	E4-5
	(4) the one and the not-one are not different	E5-147A3
	(a) it is not by otherness or on account of themselves that one is different from the not-one, and vice versa	E5-A1
	(b) they cannot be different	A1-3
b	elimination of other possible relations	A3-B3
	(1) participation ruled out	A3-4
	(2) the not-one is not a number	A5-6
	(3) nor are they part and whole	A7-B3
c	conclusion: they must be same as each other	B3-6

The first ambiguity to leap to the eye is at the beginning. Parmenides Plato) begins by establishing a premiss about auto te tauton kai to het-ron, the Same and the Other, or Different, ***themselves***. These are Forms. Then he draws therefrom a conclusion about ***things***, ouden esti tOn ontOn en hOi estin to heteron chronon oudena. auto to [whatever] is Plato's term for absolutes or Forms. Whether he means such here, or whether he means concepts (as Cornford, p. 159, suggests), is not certain. Plato seems to have made a distinction between the two (as at 143A7), which some later investigators have not. There is less question about what tOn ontOn en hOi…chronon oudeni are. If the presence of ontOn does not suffice to mark these as things, surely the reference to their duration in time does. Let us concede Plato's uncertainty about Forms, attested well enough in the introductory part of this dialogue and in unanswered contradictions to be found in the main part. Whatever Forms or dianoetic absolutes (143A7) *are*, or whatever their relations to each other are, may be questions, but there is no question that they play a role in these hypotheses. They perform a function right here in this argument. This argument aims to show us that there is a sense in which ones in the world of things are the same as others. Even common sense tells us this: they are both unities. This argument is not that the Form of the One is the same as Others, nor that one thing is the same as another, but in a third way that somehow mixes Forms (or concepts) and things: if many things or copies participate in one Form (many ones in one One, for example) it is the same Form, not another, in all of them. Or if it is concept that is meant, the same observation applies. Is this then what Parmenides' argument means here? If it is, the two hypotheses that we have so far encountered, the first and the second, divide the one analytically into Form and copy between themselves, yet the treatment of each is not wholly independent of the other. If Parmenides' treatment here of the one thing takes into account its Form or concept, we cannot help recalling that his corresponding treatment of the Form of the One, not other than the others, in the first hypothesis (139C3-D1), called upon a premiss taken from the world of things (the inverse of the situation here): only another can be other than another (139C4-5). If there are no Forms without copies, ones without others, being without not-being, and vice versa, it should not be surprising that at some point these pairs of hypotheses should depend upon one another. It is possible that they are inseparable, even when separated, and that this inseparability makes itself manifest again on the detailed level. In this argument in the context of the second hypothesis, which treats of the one being, not the One Form, Plato is talking about things, while appealing to some sort of non-things, absolutes, Forms or concepts.

g. It is like and unlike itself and others (147C1-148D4). This argument is organized somewhat asymmetrically as follows: it is

1	like the others	C2-A6
2	unlike the others	A6-C3
3	another argument, or restatement	C3-D1
4	like and unlike itself	D1-4

In section *1* the likeness of the one to the others is the likeness of their reciprocal difference. They differ from each other in the same way; they are affected alike; in this they are alike. D1-E6 is a long explanation in response to the young Aristotle's query, demonstrating that, when we say that the one is different from the others and the others are different from the one, "different" in both cases means the same thing. This first section of the argument depends upon the third section of the preceding argument (f.) that the one is different from the others (146D1-2).

Section *2* (A6-C3) refers to the fourth section of the preceding argument (the one is the same as the others, 146D5-147B6), and to the first section of this argument (the one is like the others, 147C2-148A6) for its premisses. It presumes opposite consequences from opposite premisses. If the one is like the others, because it was different from the others, then oppositely the one is unlike the others because it was the same as the others. This compounding of opposites (he began in the first section with an argument that was opposite of what we might have expected) is enough to confuse the young Aristotle, if not the rest of us.

Section *3* (C3-D1) introduces an ambiguity of a new sort. If we are quite strict, we must admit that we do not have enough evidence here to be certain whether this is a new argument, or a restatement of the two preceding sections. The first section called the one and the others, differing from one another, tauton peponthata, tauton peponthos and other inflections of these same terms, and on account of this same affect called them like: to de pou tauton peponthos homoion (148A3). This third section does the same. It is possible that the tauton peponthe (and its opposite) here (148C4-6) refers to some other affect (pathos, paschein) than that of difference, but it is not explicitly stated that such is the case. This then amounts to a restatement. But if Plato had something else in mind, it might be a new and opposite argument. Such is a possible but not a necessary inference, taking the text as it stands. This more permissive reading differs from Cornford's (*Plato and Parmenides*, p. 166).

Section *4* (D1-4) tersely applies the same sorts of reasoning as in the first three sections to the first two sections of the preceding argument (f.), 146B2-D1.

h. It touches and does not touch itself and others (148D5-149D7). This argument presents peculiar problems. First let us identify the three main sections of it, exclusive of the heading and the recapitulation:

1	it touches others and itself	D6-E4
2	it does not touch itself	E4-149A3
3	it does not touch others	A3-D5

The first section (D6-E4) is brief, and it refers for its premiss to the fourth prior section, d. (it is in itself and in another), 145B6-E6. This gives us no problem.

It is the second and third sections that give trouble. Their arguments are good enough. It is their premisses that are questionable. A premiss of the second section is that the one is not two: heOs d' an Ei hen...mEte duo einai, 149A1-3. A premiss of the third is that the one is only one, ei de ge hen monon estin, 149C4. The trouble is that it is a presupposition of this hypothesis that the one *is* two (this is precisely what distinguishes it from the first hypothesis), and it is a presupposition of the *first* hypothesis that there is only one alone. What then is wrong? Has Antiphon misremembered the conversation? Do these two sections belong in the first hypothesis? Has the text been corrupted? Or is this another instance of deliberate shuffling of assumptions? This is the only argument in the second hypothesis that did not appear in the first, excepting the slightest of references at 138A5-7. These two sections would fit well there, restoring an almost perfect symmetry. On the other hand, it must be admitted that he has mixed references to Forms and concepts into these arguments about things before (143A-144E; 146D-E), and will do so again very soon, in fact in the very next argument.

i. It is equal and unequal to itself and others (149D8-151E2). This argument is divided into five sections, and may be outlined as follows: it is

1	equal to others	D9-150E1
2	equal to itself	E1-4
3	unequal to itself	E5-151A2
4	unequal to others	A2-B7
5	all these arguments (*1—4*) are extended to discrete quantities	B7-D8

What difficulties there are, will be found mostly in the first section. These will be much alleviated if our attention is directed to three points. In the first place, the argument of the first section is a negative argument. It demonstrates that the one is equal to the others by showing that it is not unequal. to ge mEte huperchon mEte huperchomenon pollE anagkE ex isou einai, ex isou de on ison einai (150D7-8), etc. In the second place, throughout most of the argument it substitutes for unequal the terms greater or less, or greatness and smallness, meizon E elatton, megethos kai mikrotEs (passim). In the third place, it appeals for its premiss to the Forms of Greatness and Smallness and Equality. The first two points merely render this argument somewhat more complex, but the third must be the main object of our attention. Once again Parmenides (Plato) seems to be blurring the distinction between the first two hypotheses, and appealing to the nature of Forms to establish arguments about things. Notice also that such a tactic is tantamount to adopting the tactic of Socrates against Zeno in the introductory part (128E5-130A2): Forms are called upon to support an argument about things (albeit a different argument). Furthermore it raises a same assumption as was raised in one of Parmenides' criticisms of Socrates' use of Forms, namely that Forms have the physical characteristics that they are Forms of (i.e., the Form of Largeness is large; of Smallness, small; etc.; 131C12-E7, etc.). Any possible objections to such an assumption are again ignored. All of this raises more questions than it provides certainties. It is perhaps useless to try to guess what Plato was trying to do. It is better to admit that whatever else may have been the case, the relation of Forms and things, and thus of the first two hypotheses (perhaps also others), may be uncertain and paradoxical. The presence of Forms is the main point to be considered in the first section.

Section *1* (D9-150E1), equal to others, may be divided thus:

a	establishment of Forms: things are equal, greater or smaller only by their participation in such Forms	D9-A1
b	there is no Smallness in the one	A1-B7
	(1) in the whole of it	A3-B2
	(2) in part of it	B2-7
c	there is no Greatness in the one	B7-C6
d	the one, not smaller or greater than the others, must be equal to them	C6-E1

Section *2* (150E1-4), equal to itself, simply applies the same argument to the one in relation to itself.

Section *3* (E5-151A2), unequal to itself, relies upon argument d., it is in itself (145B6-C7), for the premiss. It no longer exhibits the reliance upon Forms, found in the first two sections.

Section *4* (A2-B5), unequal to others, also relies partly upon argument d., but not explicitly and this time to the second section of that argument (145C7-E3), it is in another (= others). It also relies upon an argument that the one and others are in one another (A2-9).

Section *5* (B7-E2) recognizes that greater, less and equal are measures; measures are parts; parts imply numbers. Thus the arguments of the preceding sections are extended to numbers and discrete quantities.

j. It does and does not partake of time, be and become younger and older than itself and the others (151E3-157B7). This argument is divided into two major parts:

1 the one *does* partake of time, etc.   151E3-155E3
2 the one *does not* partake of time, etc.   155E4-157B5

It is one of the arguments that seems as if it does not have a symmetrically opposite argument in the first hypothesis. This lapse of symmetry has been mentioned before, but it is perhaps appropriate that the aberrations be summarized: all the arguments are related as positives to negatives, in the first two hypotheses, except (a) the last argument of the first hypothesis is the negative of the assumption of the second; (b) the argument *h.* of the second (touch) is not to be found at all in the first, and covers both positive and negative; (c) the second arguments of each appear at first to reach similar conclusions (i.e., infinity) but really they do not, since opposite notions of infinity are at stake; (d) in the arguments of the two hypotheses about time, the One of the first is not in time, etc., while the one of the second both is and is not. There will be found, of course, a distinction, or what we have called an ambiguity, in the meaning of not being in time. This lack of opposition between the two hypotheses may be more apparent than real, but it may add to the complexities that will be noted below.

That the one does *and* does not partake of time, etc., has not always been seen as two parts of a single argument terminating the second hypothesis. To the neoplatonists, e.g. Proclus, the part *2*, 155E4-157B5 (the one does not partake of time, etc.), was a separate hypothesis. To Cornford it was a corollary to the second, which he calls hypothesis 2a. This question will be examined more closely when we come to this section of the text.

Let us take up the first part first:

1 the one *does* partake of time, etc.   151E3-155E3

    a it becomes older than itself   E6-152A5
    b it becomes younger than itself   A5-B2
    c it is older than itself   B2-D4
    d it is younger than itself   D4-E3
    e it is not and does not become   E3-10
       older and younger than itself
    f it is older than the others   E10-153B7
    g it is younger than the others   B8-D5
    h it is the same age as the others   D5-154A4
    i it does not become older or   A4-C5
       younger than the others
    j it does become younger than   C5-E3
       the others
    k it does become older than   E3-155B4
       the others
    l recapitulations   B4-C7
    m there is knowledge, opinion,   C7-E3
       sensation of it, a name for
       it, and reasoning about it

This is the most complex section of a complex dialogue. It is also the longest. Up to this point the most complicated argument has turned around two pairs of alternatives, or at the most three: positive and negative of a character in relation to self and others (e.g. like and unlike itself and others), with one case of a splitting in two of a character (e.g. unequal = greater or lesser). Here there are at least four major pairs of alternatives:

> positive and negative,
> self (one) and others,
> being and becoming,
> younger and older.

These are evident in the headings (151E3-6, 155C4-7, etc.). They result from the complex nature of time. Time presents us with its own ambiguities. Time may signify an instant or a duration, hence the attention to both being and becoming. Duration may be viewed forwards or backwards, or two times may be compared two ways, taking either as a base of reference, hence older and younger. Furthermore, an instant may be viewed as in a duration (part of time), or not (in this sense, not in time), hence the two major parts of this argument, as we shall see.

Subsections *a—d* make use of the first two of these ambiguities. *a* and *b* treat time as duration; *a*, as the normal process of aging; *b* simply reversing the viewpoint, the older in duration being younger or newer in its present state (the reference at 152A6 is to 141B1-C4). *c* and *d* view time as an instant: what *becomes* older or younger *is*, at any instant, older or younger. Starting with *e* additional ambiguities are introduced. *e* negates all the preceding four conclusions by treating time as duration, but in a different manner than heretofore: it is not comparing two separate instants in a duration, but measuring the quantity of the duration. In other words, duration is ambiguous: it is expressed by two separate instants or by the amount of time between them: you can stay from Wednesday to Friday, or three days. Whereas in *a—e* the one is any one thing, in *f* the one is a number, the first of a series of numbers. Notice that Parmenides (Plato) is also careful to distinguish others from other. In *g* the others are within the one as parts of it; elsewhere they have been externals there are references to 142D1 in 153C1, and to 145A6 and B1 in

153C2). In *h* the same age is substituted for not older or younger, i.e. a positive expression for a negative expression. The oneness of the parts of the one is now invoked (A2-4 refers to 152E10-153D5). In *i* older and younger refer to the change in difference in age, rather than difference in age (ei kai estin etc. in 154B1-2, refers to sections *f* and *g*, 152E10-153D5). *j* and *k* compare durations proportionately, instead of absolutely, as elsewhere (154C6-7 refers to 153A1-D5). *k* merely reverses *j*.

There follow two recapitulations in subsection *l*, 155B4-C7. First, subsections *i*, *j* and *k*, 154A4-155B4, are recapitulated at 155B4-C4. Then the whole section, 151E6-155B4, is recapitulated at 155C4-7.

Finally this first part ends (*m*, 155C7-E3) with the ascription of knowledge, opinion, perception, name, reasoning and all the other things that we have of the others also, just the opposite of the situation described at the end of the first hypothesis.

That brings us to the second major part of this argument:

2 the one ***does not*** partake of time, etc.,   155E4-157B5.

Let us commence by asking: what are we talking about here? Hoion dielEluthamen can mean anything. hen te on kai polla kai mEte hen mEte polla kai metechon chronou (E5-6) is the critical phrase. It modifies the subject, providing a clue to whatever the subject might be. It is the one of course, but which one? This phrase seems to establish that it is the one of the second hypothesis. It sums up its self-contradictory character very succinctly in saying that it is one and many and not one and not many, adding that it participates in time, not as an afterthought but to remind us of the immediate context, the final question about time. Unfortunately the remainder of this sentence, hoti men estin hen, ousias metechein pote, hoti d' ouk esti, mE metechein au pote ousias, clouds the issue. This predicate seems to refer to the one of the second hypothesis ***and*** the One of the first (cf. 141E9-10). So the subject seems ambiguous. It can be either the one of the second hypothesis or the one (One) of the first two hypotheses.

Thus there are two possible contexts for the ensuing discussion. But either context will do. Whether we consider change from the One of the first hypothesis to the one of the second, or change of the one of the second from contrary to contrary, in either case we have the basis for the point that Parmenides wishes to make: the one changes, and it changes in time (155E8-156A4). Various kinds of change are enumerated (A4-B8).

Parmenides' argument now follows (156C1): precisely due to the fact that it changes, the one *does not* partake of time. But it does not partake of time (note well) for quite a different reason than the reason that the One of the first hypothesis did not partake of time. There (in the first, 140E1-141D6) the One did not partake of time because of its utter transcendence of all the characteristics of existence. Here its non-participation is due to a peculiarity of change and time themselves. There seem to be three options altogether:

1. participation in time, by the one of hypothesis 2, j., *1* (151E3-155E3),

2. no participation in time, because it is utterly transcendent, the One of hypothesis 1,

3. no participation in time, because time stops in the instant of change, the one of hypothesis 2, j., *2* (155E4-157B5).

Is it possible that this last is "the third" (to triton) that Parmenides (Plato) refers to at 155E4? Whatever the answer to that question, it seems that the present argument is an integral part of the second hypothesis, and in no way represents a separate one. *Hypotheses non sunt multiplicanda praeter necessitatem.*

It exhibits the following structure:

the one changes

All of this rests upon the ambiguity of change and time as durations v.
change and time as instants. The notion of the instant was something

quite puzzling to the early Greeks, as Parmenides (Plato) makes plain right here in his extended discusssion of it (D1-E3) as a paradox. It had been the subject of one of Zeno's paradoxes about motion, i.e. the flying arrow, and it was to be the subject of Aristotle's attention in *Physics*, IV, xi. Surely the One of the first hypothesis changing to the one of the second (if it does), and even much more surely the one of the second, going through any of the numerous changes which Parmenides has just put it through, encounter this problem of change and time. It was a problem which had not in Parmenides' or Plato's time been resolved, and which deserved the attention that was called to it here.

To sum up, the second hypothesis exhibits a carefully crafted internal structure, and a structure that is (for the most part) symmetrical with that of the first hypothesis. One difference is that whereas the first denies the attribution of the contrary characters to the One, the second affirms their attribution to the one. Being contraries, their affirmation in the second requires a lengthier logical exercise. More distinctions and ambiguities are required. The hypothesis is longer. It is the longest of the eight.

Some exceptions to the complete symmetry of the two hypotheses have been noted. For the one-sided treatment of touch in the second, missing in the first, there seems to be no sure explanation. The special treatments of infinity and time are due to the peculiar and problematic nature of these. Nevertheless one can hardly finish the reading of these two hypotheses without a strong impression of their close relation. Taken together the two hypotheses emphasize the two possible states of being, and of unity: as Form and copy. The theory of Forms is not new here in Plato's writing but it receives here a problematic treatment that is new, and deeper than before. Here is a Form that does not exist! And if the one is and is not, what does "is" or "to be" mean? The fact that one thing is also many need not surprise us; it is a commonplace. But it was not so simple a matter to Plato and his contemporaries.

The remaining hypotheses will also exhibit, in pairs (3-4, 5-6, 7-8), other contradictory consequences of changes from Form to copy, or vice versa. That there are two kinds of one and two kinds of being seem now established. But there will be other problems, and we will shortly see two kinds of negation. The Form theory, the existence of Forms alongside things, raises acute problems.

THE THIRD HYPOTHESIS

The third hypothesis is much shorter than the first two. Its arguments—there are only four of them—seem quite different than any that have gone before. Parmenides (Plato) is now concentrating his attention for the first time upon a new problem, a matter that had previously been taken for granted.

a. In the first two hypotheses, the arguments about parts and wholes were used prominently, and were premises for a number of other arguments. It was a question of the One having no parts and not being a whole (first hypothesis), or of the one being a whole with parts (second). The relationship of parts and wholes itself was not questioned. At 137C5-8 it was simply accepted that a part must be part of a whole. Here in the third hypothesis this is investigated more deeply. At 157C8 it is asked, why? Pos touto; At 157C8-E2 a demonstration appears to be offered, why parts must be parts of a whole. The argument is complex and tricky (due in part to a concatenation of negatives). At the risk of being tedious, we will outline and examine this section, 157B9-E5, in detail:

1 If there are others than one, they are not
one, because they would not be others [if they
were one] epeiper alla tou henos estin, oute to
hen esti talla, ou gar an alla tou henos En.

B9

2 But the others are not entirely lacking unity   C1-2
(the one) but participate in it somehow, oude
mEn steretai ge pantapasi tou henos talla,
alla metechei pEi.

3 [Why the others somehow participate in unity]   C3-E5

    a   the others have parts; otherwise they'd be   C3-4
        one, ta alla tou henos moria echonta alla
        estin, ei gar moria mE exhoi, pantelOs an
        hen eiE.

    b   the parts are parts of a whole, moria de   C4-5
        ge, phamen (137C6), toutou estin ho an holon E

    c   the whole is one, because each of the parts   C5-8
        is not part of many parts but of a whole,
        to ge holon hen ek pollOn anagkE einai, ou
        estai moria ta moria, hekaston gar tOn moriOn
        ou pollOn morion chrE einai, alla holou
        (this too looks back to 137C6, but now the
        young Aristotle asks, why? pOs touto;).

4 [Why the whole is one, and why each of the   C8-E2
parts is part of a whole, not of many—this
is the apparent demonstration we spoke of,
answering the young Aristotle's "Why?". It
deserves close examination.]

    a   each cannot be part of a many, because, if   C8-D2
        it were, a part would somehow be part of
        itself and of each of the others, which is
        impossible, ei ti pollOn morion eiE, en
        hois auto eiE, heautou te dEpou morion estai,
        ho estin adunaton, kai tOn allOn dE henos

hekastou, eiper kai pantOn,

b [why that is impossible]   D3-7

    (1) not being a part of one (>B9), it will be   D3
           part of the others, henos gar mE on morion,
           plEn toutou tOn allOn estai,

    (2) and so it will not be a part of each one,   D4
           kai houtOs henos hekastou ouk estai morion,

    (3) and not being a part of each, it will be   D4-5
           part of none of the many, mE on de morion
           hekastou oudenos tOn pollOn estai,

    (4) being some (ti) of none of all these of   D5-7
           which it is none of any, it is impossible
           for it to be a part or anything else,
           mEdenos de on pantOn toutOn ti einai, hOn
           oudenos ouden esti, kai morion kai allo
           hotioun adunaton.

  c so the part is not a part of many or all,   D7-E2
    but of some one Idea, and of some one thing
    which we call a whole, become one completion
    of all: this is what the part is part of,
    ouk ara tOn pollOn oude pantOn to morion
    morion, alla mias tinos ideas kai henos tinos
    ho kaloumen holon, ex hapantOn hen teleion
    gegonos, toutou morion an to morion eiE.

5 Thus if the others have parts, they participate   E2-5
   in the whole and unity. The others than one
   must be one complete whole having parts, ei ara
   talla moria echei, kan tou holou te kai henos
   metechoi. Hen ara holon teleion moria echon anagkE
   einai talla tou henos.

This apparent demonstration makes use of an ambiguity of "one" (in *4, b,* (1) it is a whole; in *4, b,* (2), a part). Of more importance, its negative assumption in *4, b,* (4) begs the question: *can* a part be part of something else, namely a whole? This is just what the argument here is trying to prove, albeit in a negative way (it can't be part of a many that is not a whole; it is not a part of each; if it is not a part of each, it is a part of none, etc.) Its negative assumption (being none of all these, it cannot be a part or anything else) begs the question: can it not be part of a whole? That is something else.

The arguments about wholes and parts, it should be clear by now, are equivalent to the arguments about ones and others. Parts are and are not ones, and others; and wholes are and are not ones, and others. And wholes are and are not parts, and parts are and are not wholes, just like the ones and others in these hypotheses. The assumption first stated at 137C5-8 that parts are parts of wholes, and referred to elsewhere later, is nothing else than the assumption (ostensible conclusion) of this hypothesis that the others somehow participate in unity. Both of course are well founded on our everyday experience of things. The relations of whole and parts can be rung through all the same changes that the relations of the one and the others are run through in the eight hypotheses.

ɔ. The second argument, that the others are infinitely numerous (plEthei ɪpeira)and limited, 158B5-D8, has three sections:

1 infinite	B5-C7
2 limited	C7-D3
3 recap	D3-8

The first section, that they are infinite, commences with a reminder of he preceding argument, epei de ge pleiO henos esti ta te tou henos noriou kai ta tou henos holou metechonta…Because of this participa-ion in unity, any argument for an infinity of division, based upon a lack ɪf an atomic limit, might be suspect. Thus a different approach is used:

whatever you might wish to subtract from the many others, however small, would itself also be a plurality (C2-4), and this can be repeated indefinitely (C5-7). The subtrahend is a part, and might participate in unity, but in so far as it is not one (plEthE onta, en hois to hen ouk eni, C1), it may undergo repeated subtraction. In so far as it *is*, it is limited (the second section, C7-D3). The recapitulation (third section, D3-8) emphasizes this ambivalence: heteron ti gignesthai en autois.

c. The third argument, that the others are like and unlike each other and themselves, E1-159A6, is based upon the second, or preceding argument (b.). Since they all have the two contrary characters of infinity and limit, they have likeness and unlikeness, depending upon which are chosen for comparison.

d. The fourth argument, A6-B1, tersely extends the same reasoning to the rest of the contrary characters.

Observe: if the one is *not*, there are still others, or other ones, as here. That is the seventh hypothesis. If the One and the Others are Forms, the Others is *not* One. That is the next hypothesis, the fourth.

THE FOURTH HYPOTHESIS

The peculiarity of the fourth hypothesis which arrests one's attention is the great care with which it establishes the separateness of the One and the Others, 159B6-C4. There is no third choice, nothing that is both one and other, as the one of the second and the others of the third hypothesis were. When one has said the One and the Others, one has said it all; there is nothing else in which the One is and the Others; the One and the Others are not in the same; they are utterly separate.

All this quite emphatically marks off the fourth hypothesis from the second and the third, and applies to thoroughly separate abstractions, or Forms, as opposed to things. Furthermore, as one saw in the case of the

Form of the One in the first hypothesis, the Form of the Others also does not have the contrary characters, not any of them.

a. They are not parts or wholes, C5-D3, having no participation whatsoever in the One. The reasoning here appears to reverse itself: the non-participation of the Others in unity appears to be the conclusion of this argument, but it is really the premiss, established in the introductory part, utter separation.

b. They are not one or many, B3-E1, for the same reasons: the one and the many participate in unity, just like wholes and parts, with which they are closely associated in D6-7. Still the contrast with the third hypothesis. Furthermore they cannot be numbered (D7-E3).

c. They are not like or unlike, E2-160A3, since they would participate in unity and duality, which the preceding argument (b.) has precluded.

d. They have none of the contrary characters, A4-B2, for the same reasons.

e. B2-4 recapitulates very tersely the first four hypotheses.

The fourth hypothesis may be compared with the third, the first and the eighth. Comparisons with the third and the first have already been made. Comparison with the third requires the distinction of Forms and copies; with the first, of Forms of One and the Others. We have noted that it is emphatically pointed out that the Form of the Others has no unity whatsoever, a rather remarkable thing to say about any Form of Plato's. The fourth hypothesis therewith raises a huge question about Plato's theory of Forms. Our occasional references to this Form in the singular (the Form of the Others), as concessions to grammatical convention, sound awkward.

Comparison of the fourth with the eighth hypothesis discloses another paradox. If there is a Form of the One (fourth), the Others are utterly separate, but if there is **not** a Form of the One (eighth), the Others are not, either. Thus, while the Others and the One are utterly separate, there is some kind of a connection between them (eighth).

THE FIFTH HYPOTHESIS

If we pause to reflect upon the surprises that the hypotheses have sprung on us so far, we may recall that the first revealed a Form that does not exist; the second, a one that is many and is the subject of all sorts of contradictions; the third, many that are one; and the fourth, a Form that has no unity whatsoever. These are all remarkable revelations about Plato's metaphysics, but the fifth hypothesis is going to surprise us with yet another novelty. In it Plato addresses the question that the ancient Greeks had found the most vexing of all: can not-being be? Can that which is not, be? The real Parmenides had expressed himself rather forcibly on this question: never shall this be proven, that things which are not, are, ou gar mEpote touto damEi einai mE eonta (DK VII, line 1). Plato brought it up in the *Euthydemus*, and he offered a solution in the *Sophist*: not-to-be may mean to be different. It is a solution that applies to things perfectly well. Here in the middle of the fifth hypothesis of the *Parmenides* he meets this ontological paradox head on, without any assistance from megista genE, and proposes a different solution to a different question: can not-being be, absolutely?

The fifth hypothesis begins with a relatively long introduction, 160B5-161A5. About one quarter of the text of the hypothesis is devoted to the elucidation of what is meant here by the hypothesis, if there is not a one. The assumption here is that there is some definite idea of the one to which we ascribe not-being.

An outline of the introduction goes as follows:

1	what do we mean by this hypothesis?	B6-7
2	distinct things can ***not be***	
	a the one and the not-one	B7-C2
	b other examples, for differentiation	C2-7
3	there is knowledge of them	C7-D2
4	recap	D3-E2

5 the not-one has "thisness, thatness,   E2-7
  somethingness," etc.
6 summary: it cannot be, yet it must   E7-161A5
  participate in many (ideas)

In other words, there may be Ideas or Forms that do not exist as copies or things; in the present case, of the One. Not-being may be: what is not as a copy or thing, may be as an Idea or Form. This way of putting the connection between being and not-being puts it in terms of the kinds or modes or states of being, rather than in terms of differential negation (as in the *Sophist*).

The one that is not, is the subject of this hypothesis:

a. It has unlikeness (A6-B4) and likeness (B4-C2). Notice that the text does not say it *is* unlike or like, but that it *has* unlikeness and likeness (autO estin). (And later it does not say that it *is* unequal or equal, but that it participates, etc.) The one-that-is-not is not assumed to *be* anything yet, except an Idea (Form). Notice also that the duality of all these relations, to itself and the others, so prominent in the earlier hypotheses, has been dropped, except at 164A3.

b. It participates in inequality (C3-D1) and equality (D2-E2).

c. It participates somehow in being and not-being, 161E3-162B8. This argument is extraordinary: *1* it interrupts the pattern, established in the prior hypotheses, that goes down the list (gradually abbreviated, to be sure) of contrary characters *seriatim*; and *2* one might expect that the introduction to this hypothesis (160B5-161A5) had sufficiently established that the one-that-is-not participates somehow in being, when it ascribed to it Formal being, but apparently it had not, and here it requires restatement.

The argument is nearly entirely devoted to the *being* of the one-that-is-not. Kai mEn kai ousias ge dei auto metechein pEi, E3. Only the final line mentions its not-being. Kai mEn ousia ara, eiper mE estin, 162B7. It begins with a short section (161E4-162A1) based upon the implied premiss that truth is a kind of being. This seems not wholly unrelated to the stipulations of the introduction, 160B5-161A5, and it also foreshadows Aristotle's classification of one kind of being as truth in *Metaphysics*, E, ii—iii. Then it continues with quite a different, indeed a unique argument. We reproduce it here entire:

The one that is not, it seems, *is*, estin ara, hOs eoike, to hen ouk on, 162A1. [Here is the reason why:] ei gar mE estai mE on, alla pEi tou einai anEsei pros to mE einai, euthus estai on, because if not-being will not be, but somehow will give up being in favor of not-being, it will immediately be being, A2-3. dei ara auto desmon echein tou mE einai to einai mE on, there must be a bond [or connection] between being and not-being, ei mellei mE einai, if [not-being] will not be, A4-5, homoiOs hOsper to on to meE on echein mE einai, hina teleiOs au E, just as being has not-being not be, in order that it may completely be, A5-6, houtOs gar an to te on malist' an eiE kai to mE on ouk an eiE, because in this way being is, most fully, and not being is not, A6-7; metechonta to men on ousias tou einai on, mE ousias de tou mE einai mE on, ei mellei teleOs einai, to de mE on mE ousias men tou mE einai on, ousias de tou einai mE on, ei kai to mE on au teleOs mE estai, on the one hand, being participating in the being of being being, and in the not-being of not being not-being, if it will completely be, while on the other hand, not-being participating in the not-being of not being being, and in the being of being not-being, if it will completely not be, A6-B3. The last clause is exceedingly symmetrical, a great help in its interpretation.

The text then continues, applying these conclusions to the one-that-is-not. Summarizing, the one, if it is not, has being as well as not-being, B3-8. The role of this argument in the present hypothesis will shortly be made clear, in the next argument. Meanwhile we must observe that, taken by itself, it appears to constitute a remarkable passage in Plato's ontology.

Elsewhere, as in the *Sophist*, he addressed the question, whether not-being might be, and answered that it might be, in the Form of Difference. Here however there is no such limitation: it is absolute not-being.

d. It moves and it rests, 162B9-E3. This may be outlined as follows:

1 it moves (kinoumenon)	B9-C6
2 it rests	C6-E2
a it does not change place (metabainein)	C9-D1
b it does not turn in place (strephesthai)	D 1-5
c it does not alter (alloiousthai)	D5-8
d recap and conclusion: it rests	D8-E2
3 recap: it rests and moves	E2-3

The basis of the argument for movement is the preceding argument: if it has and has not being, it must change from one state to the other; change is motion. The basis for the argument for rest is the denial of place, and consequently motion, to what is not. At this point there is a not too troublesome confusion in the structure of Parmenides' (Plato's) arguments. The argument about motion and rest is not summed up (E2-3) until it has broached the topic of alteration (D5-8), but thereafter Parmenides takes up alteration as an independent topic.

e. It changes (alters) and does not change, E4-163A7. This is closely based upon the preceding argument: motion and alteration were closely associated, if sometimes distinguished. Their relation was an on-going problem for the ancient Greeks.

f. It does and does not come into being and pass away, A7-B6. This is based upon the preceding conclusions about change.

So, if the one is not, at least the Form is, in this the fifth hypothesis. If it were the Form that is not (sixth), there is no copy. And if the one is not, there is a Form of the Others also (seventh).

THE SIXTH HYPOTHESIS

The introduction, 163C1-D1, makes it very plain that the subject of this hypothesis is the one that is not which lacks any kind of being, oudamOs oudamE estin oude pEi metechei ousias to ge mE on, C4-5. Although it is neither Form nor copy, we listed it in the charts above of "The Eight Hypotheses" as a Form, One that is not, since, if it were a copy it would have being as a Form (hypothesis #5), but as a Form that is not, there can be no copy either.

Not being in any way whatsoever, it is neither Form nor copy, and it lacks all the contrary characters, of course. These are enumerated, it will be noticed, in the same list as in the fifth hypothesis, but in reverse order, setting aside the section on being (5., c., 161E3-162B8) which this hypothesis has addressed first of all. The arguments are simple and brief:

a. If it participates in no way whatsoever in being, it is fairly plain that it cannot come into being or pass away out of it (D1-8).

b. If it cannot become or pass away, it cannot change, since change involves those. If it cannot change, it cannot move. If it cannot be, it cannot be in the same place, i.e. rest (D8-E6).

c. If it has nothing of being, it lacks the rest of the contrary characters and everything else: greatness, smallness, equality, likeness, difference, relation to itself or others. There are no others than it, if it is not, for it to be related to, or to be like or unlike or same or different from it. It has nothing, is nothing, not this, etc., not before or after or now (E6-164B1).

d. There is no knowledge, opinion, perception, account or name of it, or anything else whatsoever having to do with beings (B1-2). There is not one, Form or thing.

We have seen just above that the comparison of the fifth and sixth hypotheses is a comparison of copy and Form of the one that is not. The fifth showed that not-being is, Parmenides (the real Parmenides, DK VIII,

1; II, 3, etc.) notwithstanding. This sixth hypothesis confirms and eluci-
dates Parmenides' dicta, where there is no Form of the One. It takes Forms
to solve the riddle. The eighth hypothesis reconfirms this: if there is no
Form of the One, there are no others, Form or copy, either.

THE SEVENTH HYPOTHESIS

The seventh hypothesis asks what has happened to the others, if there is
not a one. It is taken for granted that we speak of them, thus they exist.
They must be other than others, since they cannot be other than one.
There is no one. They cannot be other than a one which does not exist.
These others must be things, and the one that is not must be a thing.
Furthermore it is a certain particular thing, although it can be any thing.
There can be other things, of course. So we are dealing here with things,
copies, and with the differential negative. Not one thing = an other.

They appear to have the contrary characters:

a. They appear unlimited and limited	C8-165C6
1 unlimited	C8-165A5
a in number and divisibility. If one takes the smallest of them, it dissolves into many, as if in a dream, leaving only the momentary appearance of unity,	C8-D8
b they appear numerable, but that is an illusion,	D8-E3
c the smallest of them will then appear large, compared to its many divisions,	E3-165A1
d and each will appear equal to the smallest and many, as it passes from larger to smaller,	A1-5

2 they appear to have limit in respect to others, but not in respect to themselves.	A5-B4
3 recaps	B4-C6
a their continual breaking up	B4-C3
b their unlimitedness and limit	C3-6

There are three things to notice about this argument: (1) the argument about equality is out of its usual place and is one sided; it is not in accordance with the expected symmetry; (2) this is all a matter of appearance and illusion, hOsper onar en hupno (164D2), because the ones that we think that we see, and that we think the others are, keep dissolving away before our eyes; we have them only momentarily tEi dianoiai, in the mind (165A8, B6); (3) three times Parmenides (Plato) uses the word ogkos, "particle", with its very physical connotation (164D1, 165A2 and B6). These particles are things.

b. They seem like and unlike,	165C6-D4:
1 like, because, as if painted with shadows so as to produce an illusion of solidity to one looking at them from a distance, they look alike (this continues a thought broached in the preceding argument,	C6-D1 B6-C1)
2 unlike, because close up we see their difference and unlikeness to themselves (which are also others).	D1-4

The remaining attributes are merely listed:

c. same and other,	D5.
d. in touch with each other, and separate,	D5-6.
e. moving and at rest,	D6.
f. coming to be, passing away, and neither,	D7.
g. and all other such,	D8-E1.

What all this seems to be saying is that the world of things, the material world, to which any particular thing named might not belong—that the material world of all the others is continually divisible, and each of its parts divisible again and again into parts and things so small (yet still divisible) that we can no longer see them. Remember that an atomic theory was held only by a few, Democritus, et al., at the time Plato wrote this. Zeno, on the other hand, in the last of his famous four paradoxes about motion, the one about the objects (ogkoi) in the stadium, seems (to some at least) to have been arguing against the Pythagorean claim that there were indivisible smallest objects (For a concise review of this, see W. K. C. Guthrie, *A History of Greek Philosophy*, Cambridge, At The University Press, vol. II, 1965, p. 94-96). In this context Plato's use of ogkoi here may be revealing.

All these are what has happened to the others if there is not a one, one thing. The eighth and last hypothesis asks what must be the case, if it is a Form of the One that is not.

THE EIGHTH HYPOTHESIS

The assumption is that the Others is not One, nor Many: these are Forms. If they were things, the one would be others and many (hypothesis 2), and others would be one(s) (hypothesis 3). The others would also be many. A reason is given here that they are not many: in the many there would be one; if none of them are one, they are all not one, so they wouldn't be many (E5-7). But this all begs the question (and sounds very like the arguments, 157B9-E5, in the third hypothesis, and 145C7-E3, in the second). This ostensible reason is merely the negative of the assumption. It is true of things (we repeat) that there is (are) one (ones) in the many, but not of Forms. The use of ousin (E5) could be significant, if this too were not ambiguous. The conclusion, oute polla oute hen esti talla (E8), is the assumption.

The Others do not appear One or Many	(165E8-166B3).

1 They have nothing in common with   166A1-4
not-being, or not-being with them.
There is no part in not-beings.

2 Nor is there any notion (doxa) or   A4-6
phantom (phantasma) of them. One
cannot imagine any connection
between not-being and the others.

3 Therefore, if there is not a One,   A7-B2
something from the others cannot be
be or be imagined one or many. Without
one it is impossible to be many.

Following is a recap (B2-3) of the hypothesis thus far, 165E4-166B2: the Others cannot be or be imagined one or many. Parmenides (Plato) is again making use of ambiguity in this argument. The others do not and do have something in common with not-being: they are a kind of not-being. There are two kinds of negation, particular (otherness) and absolute. But is this not justified? If there is no Form of the One, there is no copy (the sixth hypothesis), and so forth. The assumptions may be about Forms here, but it appears that what is said of the Forms of the One and the Others can be applied to the copies.

There follow the contrary characters, which the others/Others do not have, in an abbreviated list. The others/Others are not:

a. like or unlike	B3-4
b. same or different	B4-5
c. in touch or separate	B5
d. nor any of the rest	B5-7
e. in short, there is nothing	B7-C2

At the end of the sixth hypothesis there was no one (or One); here there is nothing at all, no one, no others, absolute or particular.

CONCLUSION

This brings us to the final conclusion of the eight hypotheses of Parmenides' demonstration, 166C2-5: hen eit' estin eite mE estin, auto te kai talla kai pros hauta kai pros allEla panta pantOs esti te kai ouk esti kai phainetai te kai ou phainetai. "Whether there is or is not a one, it and the others, both in relation to themselves and to each other, all in every case exist and do not exist, and appear and do not appear [to do so]." Quite so. We have seen that:

(1) If there is a One, it does not exist.
(2) If there is a one, it is many.
(3) If there is a one, the others are one(s).
(4) If there is a One, the Others have nothing to do with it.
(5) If there is not a one, there is an Idea of the One.
(6) If there is not a One, the one is not in any way whatsoever.
(7) If there is not a one, there are others.
(8) If there is not a One, there are no others. There is nothing.

Of course this is all true, if one makes use of the ambiguities of being, unity and negation, and others, especially the ambiguities of particular v. absolute, or as Plato would say, copy v. Form, or, as we would also say, concrete v. abstract. And what are these? They are familiar to us as the things we touch and the ideas we have in our minds. We know that both of these kinds of things exist, each after their own fashion, just as Plato knew that they existed, only using different names for them. He evaluated the Ideas as true being. We tend to do the opposite. The argument has never been settled to everyone's satisfaction. Upon close investigation the answers to this question usually turn out to be assumptions, if not mere prejudices, certainly not compelling proof, either deductive or inductive.

Nor has the relation between Idea and copy, abstract and concrete, mind and body, been satisfactorily explained. Modern neurophysiology has only attacked half of the problem.

So we find ourselves standing where Plato stood, facing the antinomies of our primary experiences. But apparently we find those antinomies difficult to accept, and we seem to find it easier to manage the single straight-line logic which we have inherited from the Greeks, particularly Aristotle. There is no question that in many realms of our experience it works, and is the only one that works. But is this all, of life or logic?

If the *Parmenides* suggests an alternative, no one beside Plato ever left evidence that he understood it. No one ever understood the **Parmenides** literally, fully, from Plato to the present day. Most probably the present essay is only one more step in a progression initiated by Cornford in 1939 toward a full understanding. But these steps will, let us hope, convince readers to take the *Parmenides* seriously and literally.

Looking backward one final time, if we ask, how did Plato come to write this dialogue? an answer is at hand. The title provides the clue. The dialogue is perhaps the third of the three projected by Plato in the *Sophist* 254B, and the *Statesman* 257-258, third at least in dramatic order. In any case, Parmenides (witness Plato's encomium in the *Theaetetus* 183E) was certainly Plato's hero as a philosopher, and the *Parmenides* dilates upon precisely the problem raised by Parmenides himself. His One, although he had no other name for it, was what Plato called a Form, what we call an abstraction. In his time and after, no one understood this, except Plato. And then no one understood Plato—that in the **Parmenides** he expanded this discovery. Everyone understood Parmenides' One as the immobile, indivisible universe, that is in a material mode, and the *Parmenides* as some kind of game, if not as some kind of metaphor. Plato was not above games and myth now and then, but these evaluations of Parmenides and the *Parmenides* are travesties. How can we be so naive as to believe in them any longer?

Claremont, California
September 30, 1989
Revised 12/4/01

A COMMENTARY ON ARISTOTLE'S METAPHYSICS

CONTENTS

A COMMENTARY ON ARISTOTLE'S METAPHYSICS

INTRODUCTION

However it may have been put together, we should be able to read Aristotle's *Metaphysics* as one book with a unified structure in which all or most of the parts play a significant role. The following studies aim to elucidate that structure. Even if the book was assembled by some person or persons known or unknown in the centuries just before or after the beginning of the Christian era, whoever did so must have had some reason for considering it as a single sensible whole. What is more, they were two thousand years closer to Aristotle than we are, and common sense dictates that their attribution of the text, directly or indirectly, must not be without some creditable foundation. Then the question to be asked is simply, what was Aristotle in the *Metaphysics* trying to say, altogether and in its parts?

How can one answer this question? Discounting what *we* think the text means, how can we find some objective evidence in the text itself for what Aristotle may have meant? What method will give us some assurance that we are finding what *he* meant, not just what we think he meant? The method used here is adapted from an old suggestion that you may recall learning long ago, perhaps somewhat reluctantly, from your school teachers. Before commencing to write a composition, they told us, organize what you have to say. Let us invert that suggestion. Taking something that someone else has written, if we find that it exhibits organization, structure, in its thought, let us infer that the writer planned his composition, that he considered it carefully, and that the resulting structure is a clue is what he meant to say. A clear structure would seem to be objective internal evidence of planning and intention. This is the technique we aim to use in approaching the *Metaphysics*. If we can find evidence of a rational plan in its parts and as a whole, we conclude that this is objective evidence of what Aristotle wanted to say, not just what we think he meant. That the shape is really there, and is not just a figment of our imagination, will be shown below.

This approach will be applied on three different levels.

(1) It will be applied to the treatise as a whole. Does it exhibit a rational structure from beginning to end? (2) It will be applied to individual books, and to selected difficult passages within some of these books. (3) It will be asked, does the treatise as a whole fit appropriately in a larger context?

There are some difficulties in any approach to a text like this, which deserve brief mention at the outset. First there is the vast cultural gap that separates us from Aristotle and his contemporaries. The questions they asked may seem silly to us at times, having to do with matters we have long taken for granted. But they were the first to ask such questions, and it is usually thanks to their investigations that we can now take such matters for granted. A respect for their accomplishment may assist us with our own questions. A sort of childishness is in order when we return to the texts of ancient Greece.

Secondly, the language is simple, and above all it is plastic. The technical vocabulary that was established by later generations (especially Cicero) is lacking. What we call "matter," for example, Aristotle called "out of which," ex hou. Furthermore, terms are not yet fixed, but various and changing. Aristotle recognized this. The ambiguity of words is one of the main themes of the *Metaphysics*. He made a beginning in dealing with the problem.

Finally, the language is Greek. I would like to persuade you that the understanding of ancient Greek is not an insuperable difficulty. Just the opposite: you may find it a source of pleasure. So another aim of these papers is to use bits and pieces of the Greek text to assist you in coming to know something about the ancient Greek language, if you are not familiar with it, or to persuade you to return to the Greek text, if you are. This study was first conceived as an exercise in learning the language. For the purposes of understanding ancient philosophy, it is surprising what a long way knowledge of even a few phrases will go. Their repetition here, and the presence of a few short quotations, couched in proper contexts, may give the reader a useful introduction to an important and exciting language. At the same time it brings us to the bed-rock foundation of our evidence. The last is by far the most important point. I am grateful to my former teacher, Philip Wheelwright, for the pungent observation (*pace* Alexander Pope) that "You know, it is surprising how far a little Greek will take you."

A SHORT OUTLINE OF THE
WHOLE OF THE METAPHYSICS

I. Introductory and propaedeutic books

A. The nature and value of knowledge	Α	or	I
B. The causes	A, a		II
C. Problems	B		III
D. Language, logic and metaphysics	Gamma		IV
E. Definitions	Delta		V
F. What kind of science do we seek?	E, 1		VI

II. The three ontologies

A. The conceptual ontology, or internal
    ontology of matter and form

1. kinds of pure being	E, 2	
2. accidental being and being as truth dismissed	E, 2-4	
3. being of the categories: ousia	Z, H	VII, VIII
4. being as potentiality and actuality	Theta	IX

B. The ontology of the One	I	X

C. The quasi-physical ontology, or
    the external ontology of the
    Unmoved Prime Mover

1. recap of A-E, and extracts from the *Physics*	K	XI
2. recap of the conceptual ontology, and the introduction of motion	Lambda, 1-5	XII
3. motion and the Unmoved Prime Mover	6-10	

III.   Appendices on numbers

   A. Numbers and abstractions, the   M   XIII
     theory of Ideas
   B. Numbers and opposites; the physical   N   XIV
     world; Plato's lectures

The individual examination of the several books will gradually reveal their place in such a structure. Book A, after a preamble on the nature and value of knowledge, raises immediately one of Aristotle's major original contributions to thought: the theory of the four causes. Book a ("little alpha") is an integral part of this discussion. Instead of seeing these two books as some sort of a history (A) followed by some sort of an excurse added by a student (a), we should see them as two parts of a discussion of a single topic, the four causes. These lay the cornerstone of his metaphysics and of the *Metaphysics*. Books Beta, Gamma and Delta (III, IV, and V) also have something in common. They all raise problems to be considered before launching the main investigation. Book Beta does so explicitly. Books Gamma and Delta do the same, if not so explicitly. They are discussions of linguistic problems (pollachOs legetai, peri tou posachOs), as in retrospect those of B turn out to be. Thus the main purport of the introductory part of this investigation, after laying the cornerstone, is to demonstrate the difficulties in the tools used in its pursuit: the terms, their ambiguities. These ambiguities will be seen to be due partly to the primitive state of the language, and partly to difficulties inherent in the subject itself. How clear some of the latter were to Aristotle is hard to say. They will become clearer to us as we proceed.

So much for the introductory books. They end with E, i, and comprise a distinct section of the treatise, with a propaedeutic character.

The main body of the treatise comprises Books E, ii—Lambda. Much discussion has been devoted to the heterogeneity of these books. Philip Merlan spoke of a *metaphysica generalis* and a *metaphysica specialis*; others, of a metaphysics (E—Theta, more or less) and a theology (Lambda). Books I and K are often disregarded (I) or repudiated (K). There seems to be disappointment that it does not all hang together as one single system. But it does, and this is all unnecessary. E, ii—Lambda constitute a single ontological inquiry, with complementary parts. These are three in number.

First of all let us deal with Book I, the middle one. It stands by itself as an undertaking to deal with a traditional ontology inherited by Aristotle from his predecessors, chiefly Plato and Parmenides. It is rejected ultimately, when Aristotle arrives at his own definition of unity, one that dissolves the obvious inadequacies of prior speculation. In is conceivable that Book I could have been positioned elsewhere in Part II of the outline above, but it belongs there somewhere. Perhaps its actual intervention between the other two ontologies has deceived us somewhat.

The other two ontologies comprise the main body of Aristotle's constructive metaphysics. They are the ontolgies proper. That they are two, instead of one, should neither surprise us nor discomfort us. Their duality reflects the duality in Aristotle's original assumptions here: in the four causes. These divide naturally into two pairs. Form and matter comprise one pair. Aristotle's first ontology in E, ii—Theta, is devoted to them. We have called this an internal or conceptual ontology, because he seems to be trying to conceptualize, without reference to movement, what constitutes "things" or whatever is. He pursues abstractions, on hE on and ousia, that are constituents.

The other pair are the moving and final causes. Books Kappa and Lambda are devoted to them. It is a quasi-physical ontology. Having to do with movement, it borders closely on a physics, in fact on the *Physics*. It is also characterized by the aspect of externality found in the moving and final causes, especially when compared with the first ontology.

There is another way of explaining this duplication of ontologies. We will discover, even though Aristotle does not notice this explicitly, that two other important words in his vocabulary have, each of them, a double meaning. These important words are chOris (outside, beyond) and akinEton (unmoved, motionless). As a result, the separate, motionless being which is the object of his inquiry may be found in either of two places, (1) in our minds or (2) beyond the heavens, i.e. (1) as a mental abstraction or (2) as the Unmoved First Mover, ho prOtos ouranos. The two ontologies reflect this ambiguity.

The one book, K, is problematical: it seems like some sort of recapitulation of what has gone on before, followed by a conscious reorientation in a physical direction. Thus the extracts from the *Physics*. But it seems withal like an ill-done insertion, at the same time that it seems to belong here if it belongs anywhere. Book Lambda does a better job of recapitulation and transition in its first five chapters. The last five chapters of it are the heart of the quasi-physical, or external ontology.

This leaves the last two books, M and N. They are two appendices. Like Iota, they deal with some current speculations that had to be disposed of. These are much newer than the theories of unity, but not entirely unrelated to them. They are the theories of number that still had a place in the Academy in the late fourth century, some clearly inspired by Plato. M deals with numbers and abstractions; N, with numbers and opposites. Or respectively they deal (M) with the theory of Ideas and (N) with Plato's "Unwritten Doctrine" or lectures.

In the detailed discussions that follow, the reader is urged to refer back frequently to the outline that stands at the head of this section, to keep reminded where the individual books fit in the structure of the whole. In several instances the details will carry us far from the overall view, inasmuch as the *Metaphysics* presents us many difficult textual problems. These must be and can be straightened out, if we are to make sense of this text.

BOOK A
KNOWLEDGE AND THE CAUSES

One may outline the first book of the *Metaphysics* thus:

A. The value and nature of knowledge, especially   chapter i
   the knowledge of universals and causes

B. What kinds of causes?   ii
  1. universal and first causes
  2. the beginnings of philosophy

C. The four original causes   iii-vii
  1. the summary list of the four causes   iii
    a. hE ousia kai to ti En einai (formal)
    b. hE hulE (material)
    c. hothen hE archE tEs kinEseOs (moving)
    d. to hou heneka kai tagathon (final)
  2. what our predecessors had to say about them
    a. material cause (983b6)
     1 monists (b20)
     2 pluralists (984a8)
    b. moving cause (a18)
     1 monists denied motion, except Parmenides (a27)
     2 pluralists (b5)
    c. recap and criticism (985b10)   iv
    d. other causes   v
     1 Pythagoreans
     2 Eleatics (986b8-987a2)
      a Parmenides, logical (formal?)
      b Xenophanes and Melissus don't fit the scheme

      3 another recap; the Pythagoreans begin
          to introduce the formal cause (a13-28)

      4 Plato   vi

    e. recap: how the four causes were found,   vii
       and no others

  3. critique of these theories   viii-ix
    a. monists
    b. pluralists (989a19)
    c. Pythagoreans (929b29)
    d. Plato   ix

D. Conclusion: the four causes and no others   x
   were sought by our predecessors
   1. imperfectly
   2. individually they didn't contribute much; a,i collectively they did.

Such an outline reveals the main topic of Book A. It is not "the predecessors" (hoi proteron hEmOn) or Plato, for example, even though these seem to preempt our attention (two whole chapters on Plato alone). The structure of the book points to something else.

The main topic of A is the causes. They are the point of the introductory chapters (i, ii) on knowledge and wisdom. They provide the *raison d'être* of the inquiry into the doctrines of the predecessors, and they are the conclusion of that inquiry. The book ends with them in chapter x, as it began with them, and refers to them frequently in between. The following book, little alpha, continues with them.

If asked to sum up in a few lines the purport of Book A, what would we say? Would it not be: "The highest science, the science we seek [metaphysics], is the science of the four causes that were enunciated already in the *Physics*. These and these only were sought, imperfectly, by our predecessors. They are the object of our search?"

Does the rest of the *Metaphysics* fulfill this expectation? At first sight it seems not. To be sure, the causes are mentioned often, but who has made them the basis for a coordinated structure of the treatise as a whole? Books Zeta and Eta treat of matter and form, and Lambda, of the Prime Mover, but who has viewed these as complementary rather than as conflicting? The tendency has been to prefer one or the other: a general metaphysics or a special; or an ontology of form and matter or a theology. But if our first science is the search for the original causes, and there are four of these, then it should not surprise us if it found the four upon a somewhat equal footing. This in fact it does, if one reconsiders the matter. It takes them in pairs. The main body of the treatise, we saw, comprises three ontologies. One of these, a traditional one inherited from Plato, Parmenides and others, about the One, is examined and found wanting. It is rejected. That leaves (1) the ontology of ousia, and (2) the ontology of the Prime Mover. But (1) ousia is divided into matter and form, and (2) the Unmoved Prime Mover links the moving cause with the final cause (1072b1-4). Thus the two pairs of causes provide the overall framework of the *Metaphysics*, and the promise of A is fulfilled. The two ontologies are complementary. A balanced view is provided by serious attention to Book A as not a casual but an organic introduction to the whole. The treatise as a whole will emphasize the four causes in not one, not four, but two ontologies which take them in pairs.

Here are a few notes on details of Book A:

Chapter i, 981a13-27: Aristotle, comparing and evaluating experience and art here, declares that experience is based upon particulars, while art and knowledge are based upon the conception of a universal. Then he goes on to evaluate the two, experience and art, and he declares that sometimes experience is better than art, as in practical affairs, but that there is more knowledge and understanding in art than in experience. The point that should claim our attention is that here at the very beginning of the *Metaphysics* Aristotle reveals a very balanced appreciation of both the particular and the universal. There is not here the preference for particulars, that he is sometimes reputed to have. Chapter ii, 982a9, 22, 24, contains more of the same.

Chapter v, 986b8-987a2, on the Eleatics, especially Parmenides, Melissus and Xenophanes: this passage deserves very careful consideration. Comparing the various traditions, first the pluralists are dispensed with (986b8-10). Then the remaining phusiologoi are distinguished from the Eleatics. Both these groups were monists (peri tou pantos hOs mias ousEs phuseOs apephEnanto), but the former instituted motion to generate the universe, while the latter made it motionless (ekeinoi men gar protitheasi kinEsin, gennOntes ge to pan, houtoi de akinEton einai phasin—b16-17). But that's not all. Among the Eleatics there is a further distinction made. Melissus treated the One in a material manner (kata tEn hulEn); Parmenides, in a logical way (kata ton logon—b18-20). Finally, even Parmenides himself was forced to see it two ways, logically supposing being to be one, but the sensible world to be many (b27-33), to hen men kata ton logon pleiO de kata tEn aisthEsin hupolambanein einai (b31-33). This distinguishes Parmenides from the other Eleatics. It shows that Aristotle was aware of the peculiar role he played in proposing a different sort of unity and being, a sort not physical. But he doesn't dwell on it.

Chapter v, 987a20-27: this gem of an argument reminds us of the dialectic of Plato's *Parmenides*. The essence of the double cannot be the same as the essence of two, or if so then the essence of the single would likewise be the same as the essence of the one, in which case the one would be many, which is impossible! This is an illustration of how the Pythagoreans made a mistake in taking the first thing used for a definition, for the substance of the thing defined. Two is not the substance of the double, even though it is the first thing used for the definition of it. We are also reminded of the first hypothesis of the *Parmenides*.

Chapter viii, 989b29-990a32: it should not surprise us that much of this passage is so difficult to understand. We know so little about the topical reference here: the Pythagoreans.

A (LITTLE ALPHA)

Whatever the origin of this book, it fits appropriately in the scheme of the whole of the *Metaphysics*. It consists of three chapters. The first chapter seems to complete the thought of Book A, and to belong with that book. One might sum it up as follows: individually the predecessors did not contribute much, but collectively they did; our debt to them is great, regardless of whether we agree with their opinions, or not; the search for truth is the search for the causes and absolutes. This is a recap of Book A.

The third chapter (to have done with it) of a is short, and consists of a few seeming gratutitous remarks on method: familiarity is an aid to knowledge, and the province of exactitude is the non-material. The end of the chapter is quite suspect. So far that looks like a bit of a grab bag, not very helpful to our thesis.

It is the second chapter that is the crux of Book a. It too doesn't appear helpful at first. It is one of the most difficult chapters of the entire *Metaphysics*. But close study will reveal it to be a highly organized and meaningful text, one that places it right in line with Book a, continuing and concluding the discussion of the four causes. After the introduction and discussion of the four causes in A and a, i, Aristotle here in a, ii, takes up a question of no small importance for his first science: are any of the causes infinite in number, or not? Of course they are not, he states at the outset (994a1-2). He goes on to show this in respect to two kinds of limit: A., of succession, and B., of kind, (A. eis euthuOrian and B. kat' eidos) 994a2). This is the purpose and content of chapter ii. We give first an outline and then a detailed gloss of the text, in order to demonstrate this contention, and the places that this chapter and this book take in the structure of the whole.

The causes, writes Aristotle, are not infinite:

A. In succession (eis euthuOrian)   994a3

   1. summary statement a3
      a. not the material cause (oute hOs ex hulEs…)   a3
      b. not the moving cause (oute hothen,…)   a5
      c. not the final cause (oude to ou heneka…)   a8
      d. nor the formal (kai epi tou ti En einai…)   a10

   2. detailed argument (*order changed*)   a11
      b. moving cause (tOn gar mesOn…)   a11
         1 upwards (epi to anO…)   a11
         2 downwards (epi to katO…)   a19
      a. material cause (dichOs gar…)   a22
        (misplaced fragment—see below)   b6-9
      c. final cause (epi de to hou heneka…)   b9
      d. formal cause (alla mEn oude…)   b16

B. In kind (kat' eidos)   b27
  (very brief)

The opening summary statement is fairly straightforward and easy. The difficult part of the text begins with the detailed argument showing why the causes are not infinite "in succession," at 994a11, tOn gar mesOn. The text takes up the demonstrations in a different order than that in which they were first summarily presented. It begins with the argument with respect to the moving cause. It does not label it as such, but the content of the argument makes this quite clear, and furthermore, the other three arguments with respect to the other three causes *are* clearly labelled (one of them perhaps causing us a moment's difficulty in recognizing it, but let us take that up when we come to it). That leaves us the moving cause for consideration at this point (994a11).

The discussion here of the moving cause is divided into two parts, looking, as it were, in two directions: *1* upwards, epi to anO, or toward the origin (the first cause), and *2* downwards, epi to katO, or toward the present (the proximate cause), mechri tou nun. Again, the first part is not labelled, but is clear from the content of the argument. The second part is labelled explicitly, as well as clear from the content. It begins at 994a19 and ends on line 22, at which point the argument with respect to the material cause is taken up.

There is one more difficulty: it looks as though lines 994b6-9, hama de kai adunaton …mE aidion einai, have slipped out of place, and belong in line 994a19 at the conclusion of the first part of the discussion of the moving cause. They certainly make more sense there. Now acting on this hypothesis, and before proceeding any further, let us attempt to translate this text of the first argument, respecting the moving cause, doing so rather literally for the sake of precision rather than style.

"Because: of intermediates [causes] of which there are some last and some prior, there must be a prior cause of those from it. For, if we must say which of the three is the cause, we say the first. Not the last; the final one is [the cause] of none [of the intermediates]. Nor the middle, for [it is only the cause] of one. It makes no difference if there is one or many [middles], nor [if] infinite or finite. Of infinite [middles] in this sense, and generally of the infinite, all the middle members up to the present [may be treated] in the same manner. So if there is no first, in all there is no cause."

Picking up now the misplaced fragment, 994b6-9, hama de kai…aidion einai: "At the same time it is impossible for the first eternal cause to perish. For if the coming-to-be is not infinite in the upward direction, it is necessary that, that from which first something came to be perishing (a genitive absolute), that which came to be [from it] is not eternal" (or possibly: "that from which something first came to be perishing, it could not be eternal." The first seems to make more sense, but the second alternative seems grammatically possible).

Now returning to line 994a19, alla mEn oud' epi to katO: "Nor can it go to infinity in the downward direction, having a beginning in the upward, as from fire water, from this earth, and thus always another kind coming into being."

If the above translation is somewhat inelegant, it is for the sake of the attempt to render as faithfully as possible the meaning of the Greek text. In the last words, concluding his discussion of the moving cause, Aristotle seems as if reminded of the material cause, to which he turns next, dichOs gar gignetai tode ek toude, 994a22.

The words tode ek toude plainly label the material cause, as they did in 994a3 just above: oute gar hOs ex hulEs tod' ek toude dunaton ienai eis apeiron. The substance of the text, 994a22-b6, also plainly has to do with the material cause. Passing the textual difficulties in lines 22 and 23, about which the two best editors, Ross and Jaeger, disagree, but which make lit- tle difference, we are then given the two ways that the material cause may work: (1) like the man out of the growing child, and (2) like air out of water. In lines 25-31 immediately following, the difference is explained: (1) in the first case there remains a subsistent medium, aei gar esti metaxu. (2) In the second, there does not; the original material disappears, phtheiromenou thaterou. Then in lines a31-b3 Aristotle makes another important distinction: (1) the first example of the cause is not reversible, while (2) the second is. You cannot make a boy out of a man, but you can (in his physical doctrine) make air out of water and then turn it back into water (in the text, it may be noted, he has just done so, lines 994a24 and 30-31 being closely compared). Now the point of all this is (994b3-4): in neither case is it possible to continue infinitely, amphoterOs de adunaton eis apeiron ienai.. And finally the reasons: (1) in the first case the subsis- tent medium constitutes a limit; (2) in the second, the process is reversible.

The precise structure of the above argument is highlighted grammatically by the succession of three men...de periods, following the initial E...E period. At 996b4 then we have the interruption recalling the moving cause, which we suggested above be removed to a more appropriate place.

Aristotle turns to the final cause at 994b9 with the words, epei de to hou heneka telos . There is no difficulty in understanding his argument here.

With the words, alla mEn oude to ti En einai, b16, the going gets difficult again. As with the other causes, so with the formal: the essence cannot be referred to another definition, multiplying the explanations. The first or most immediate definition of a series is best, aei te gar estin ho emprosthen mallon...What he seems to have in mind here is a series such as "Socrates is a man; a man is a rational animal; a rational animal is a living being, etc," that is, an ascent through the species and genera to the ultimate categories.

With the words, eti to epistasthai anairousin hoi houtOs legontes ("and they do away with certain knowledge who speak thus", 994b20) there seems to be a slight change in the argument. Eti usually signifies the introduction of a new point, in Aristotle's texts, and there is a new idea introduced here: ta atoma. But what does houtOs mean? Does houtOs, "thus," refer (1) directly to the immediately preceding argument which we have just explained? (2) Or to a wholly new idea? (3) Or indirectly to the preceding argument, with the introduction of some nuance in thought? And what are ta atoma? Are they (a) the first and immediate definitions only, hoi emprosthen? Or (b) the successive members of the series referred to above? Or (c) the ultimate, indissolvable elements of the series, such as the categories themselves (substance, quality, quantity, etc.)?

Since Aristotle says here that "they do away with certain knowledge who speak thus, because they *cannot* know (emphasis mine) until they have reached the indivisibles," ou gar hoion te eidenai prin eis ta atoma elthein 994b21), the first choices, (1) and (a), seem to be eliminated. Nor does the thought seem to be wholly new (2); nor do the successive members of the series fit the notion of ta atoma (b). Aristotle seems best understood here as referring to (c) the ultimate elements of the series, that he has mentioned, the categories (cf. Liddell, Scott, Jones, *A Greek-English Lexicon*, 1940, p. 271, and the text below, 995b29, 998b16, etc.) and thus (3) grafting a new thought onto the old one.

Since the knowledge that Aristotle has just been discussing is certain knowledge, scientific knowledge, to epistasthai, he now subjoins a remark that there will be no perceptive knowledge either. "How can one perceive things that are indefinite in such a manner," kai to gignOskein ouk estin, ta gar houtOs apeira pOs endechetai noein (994b21-23)?

Following this there is a very recondite allusion, which was probably suggested to Aristotle by his use of the words, atoma and apeira. It might easily be passed without notice. He says, "It is not like the line (ou gar homoion epi tEs grammEs), which never stops being able to be divided, but if one does not stop, it is not known (994b23-24)." This does *not* mean that it is not like the line in that progress toward the infinite must be stopped for there to be knowledge of it. In *that* respect it *is* like the line. He means that in the case of definition one must stop with the *first* one, and not do any further dividing, rather than stop at some arbitrary point later in the process of division. Why this odd and cumbersome expression? He gives himself away when this metaphor of the line momentarily arrests his attention, so that he adds parenthetically: "on which account one who is traversing the infinite does not count the sections," dioper ouk arithmEsi tas tomas ho tEn apeiron diexiOn (b24-25). This is a plain reference to his solution of Zeno's Dichotomy problem in *Physics*, VIII, viii, 263a26-30, that you can traverse a line that is infinitely divisible, but not if you stop to count the divisions.

The next sentence has caused further difficulty. Bonitz (as quoted by Ross), Ross and Jaeger all disagree on the text as well as the meanings. Alla kai tEn hulEn *en* kinoumenOi? Alla kai tEn holEn *ou* kinoumenOi? a corruption? An intrusion of a marginal note? Whichever the case, the meaning seems clear, when taken as a continuation of the immediately preceding thought, as a reference to the allusion to Zeno's problem: "it is necessary to know the material substrate (i.e. the line), or the whole (i.e. the whole line) in any movement, and to be in no infinite. If not, the essence of the infinite is not infinite," ei de mE, ouk apeiron g'estin tOi apeirOi einai (b25-27). This last line, concluding this section of the text, means, as pointed out in the *Physics, loc.cit.* that the infinity of divisibility only exists potentially when one traverses a line, not actually.

This whole difficult passage is coherent and meaningful within the larger context. Most interesting is this recall of a highlight of the *Physics*, to set up a distinction from his topic of the moment, in an effort to make that topic clearer: not seeking a succession of divisions of a definition, i.e. not defining *ad infinitum*, is not a problem we solve in the same way we solved the problem of a continuum in the *Physics*. This, he is in effect saying, is different.

That concludes the argument that the causes are not infinite in succession (A.). Aristotle then turns to the second main division of this chapter, the argument that the causes are not infinite in kind, kat' eidos. The argument, five lines long, 994b27-31, is brief, and presents no problem. Thus ends this difficult second chapter, which is the main portion of Book a.

Whatever the origin of a, it fits appropriately, as we said before, in the scheme of the *Metaphysics*. Aristotle, having determined that the science he was seeking, the first science, was a science of the four causes, found it important to demonstrate that the search for them would have an end, that the subject was a finite subject. In the speculative tradition he inherited, moreover, the limit and the unlimited were primary principles of long standing, about which there had been much discussion. It should not surprise us that he saw fit to address these at length, near the very beginning.

BETA
PROBLEMS

The place of Book B in the structure of the treatise as a whole is amply explained by Aristotle in the first seventeen lines of the book (995a24-b4).

The structure of the book itself is made plain by the serial listing of the problems in brief (995b4-996a17) in the remainder of the first chapter, and the serial discussion of each in detail in the remaining five chapters. There is a slight discrepancy of order, and an addition of one problem in the detailed discussion, but none of this poses any difficulty. Also the several individual problems are clearly marked by introductory tag phrases, such as poteron…, esti d' aporia…, aporEseien an tis…, etc., and the internal dialectical structure of most (not all) of the problems is marked by recurrent tags, such as mias men…alla mEn ei, ei men…ei de, etc.

The style of the detailed treatments of the problems varies. Does not this suggest that this may not be just a series of scholastic exercises? Some matters of wide-spread discussion are to be seen among these problems, for example: the status of immaterials such as Ideas and mathematicals, the nature of to ti En einai, the requisites of knowledge, Zeno's doctrines, the nature of points, lines and surfaces. There seems little doubt that this list reflects contemporary discussion and argument.

We should take care not to lose sight of the forest because of the trees. It is not only the particulars of each problem that should concern us, but the underlying causes of perplexity. Often these are recurrent, and the problems differ chiefly only in their linguistic dress. So it is with the dilemma about substance: is it sensible, material, perishable, individual (4, 8, 10, 12, using the summary list at the beginning of the first chapter, and the extra or fifteenth problem in the detailed list at the end of chapter vi), or is it something other than such tOn deuro objects? What is the relation between these two kinds, in Aristotle's mind? In the minds of his contemporaries? In ours? Are the questions dealing with genera and elements (6, 7, 9) or with kind and number (9, 11) related? There would seem to be some relation between the second problem and those that deal with the relation of sensibles (etc.) and non-sensibles. The eleventh and the fourteenth problems are derived from well-known doctrines of Parmenides, the Pythagoreans and Plato about the nature of being, the One and mathematicals. What are their relations with Ideas and the others?

There seems to be an underlying context to all these problems. They seem like facets of a half-seen underlying general difficulty, or like particular difficulties of actual experience that Aristotle is about to gather up into one investigation and a single treatment: what is the relation of the things we reach with our minds and the things we can touch with our hands?

The first, second and thirteenth (potentiality) problems seem especially originally Aristotelian, and seem to suggest his own contibution to the unravelling of those other problems. The causes, the foundations of logic, and the "other meanings" of potentiality are Aristotle's inventions. The causes mean of course the two pairs, matter and form, and moving and final. These provide us the keys to the structure of the *Metaphysics*. It was around them that Aristotle formed a comprehensive solution to all the superficially heterogeneous problems. It was not in the individual replies that are often carefully searched out for us, interesting as these may be in themselves.

To recapitulate, Book B is not just a collection of little problems. It is an exploration of the facets of one great problem. It was Aristotle's genius that he was able to see them as such, and to deal with them as such in the treatment that follows.

There are a few particular passages in Book B that deserve special comment:

B, i, 995b4-6; ii, 996a18-b26: Books A and a have established that the causes meant here by Aristotle are quite specific, i.e. the famous four, form, matter, moving and final (A, iii, 983a26-32, etc.). This is worth recalling here, since it is around just these that "the science we seek" will be structured, in the ontologies of (1) Z, H, and Theta, and (2) K, Lambda.

B, i, 995b20-27, etc., pros de toutois peri tautou kai heterou kai enantiotEtos, kai peri proterou kai husterou kai tOn allOn hapantOn tOn toioutOn, etc.: what are these lines talking about? What is their relation to sumbebEkota kath' hauta? And what are these latter? To begin with the second question, Ross in his note to these lines (*Aristotle's Metaphysics*, Oxford, 1924, p. 224) *distinguishes* "same, other, like, unlike," etc. from the sumbebEkota kath' hauta. I disagree. Just the contrary. These are examples of sumbebEkota kath' hauta, as the term is used here. The issue comes down to this: what does pros mean here in line 20? Does it mean "beside, in addition to" or something separative like that, as Ross seems to read it? Or does it mean "along with, among" these or something inclusive like that? Perhaps the answer is suggested by our first question above. What are these lines talking about? What are these terms, "like, unlike" etc.? They are some of the tanantia of Plato's *Parmenides*, the repetitive list of opposites. The inclusion of enantiotEtos (line 21) simply sums it up, after mention of two particular pairs in that list. Lines 25-27 add a comment: these predicates are not just individual members of any old list, but are part of the list of opposites under the headings of the one and the many, hen heni enantion, i.e. the tanantia of the *Parmenides*, and no doubt also of active tradition (peri hosOn hoi dialektikoi, etc.). In short the sumbebEkota kath' hauta here are the list of tanantia that Plato refers to in the *Parmenides* and elsewhere, and these are what Aristotle is talking about in these lines, giving some examples, though not the complete list.

B, ii, 996b10-26 (first problem): this is a detailed statement of the claims of a science of each of three of the four causes for prior consideration as the first science. he men ...(lines 10-13) states the claims of the final cause; hE de.... (lines 13-22), the formal; peri de...(lines 22-26), the moving cause. The material cause would appear to be ignored.

B, i and iii, 995b29; 998b16 and b29; 999b12 and b15, etc. (seventh problem): in a, ii, 994b21 we identified ta atoma with the highest categories. Liddell, Scott, Jones, p. 271, concur, and Bonitz, *Index Aristotelicus*, p. 120, admits the possibility with a question mark, "(?)," near the top of the right hand column. Here however it seems to suggest individuals (995b29, 998b16), or possibly the lowest species (999a12 and 15). PollachOs legontai ta atoma.

B, iii, 998b22-27 (seventh problem): Aristotle has just remarked that on and hen are the first genera, and most of all are predicated of all things. Continuing, he then says ouk hoion te de tOn ontOn hen einai genos oute to hen oute to on, there cannot be one (highest, or first) genus of beings, either One or Being, anagkE men gar tas diaphoras hekastou genous kai einai kai mian einai hekastEn, because on the one hand it is necessary that the differentia of each genus (i.e. of those just named, One and Being) are and are one, each of them. adunaton de katEgoreisthai H ta eidE tou genous epi tOn oikeiOn diaphorOn E to genos aneu tOn autou eidOn, but on the other hand it is impossible either for the species to be predicated of the genus on its own differences i.e. you can't predicate unity of being, if you are going to predicate being of unity), or the genus [to be predicated] without its own species i.e. being without unity, unity without being, etc.), hOst' eiper to hen genos E to on, oudemia diaphora oute on oute hen estai, so whether the One is a genus, or Being, neither will be a difference, neither Being nor One. If this passage is difficult to understand, as well as to translate, perhaps the situation that Aristotle is here describing can be illuminated by the following diagram:

```
genera:        hen        on
              /  \       /  \
differences:  hen  on   hen  on
```

Being both is and is one, and One both is and is one. Neither can be the highest genus alone, without the other. This is Aristotle's way of showing, reversed, what Plato had shown in the first hypothesis of the *Parmenides*: an Absolute One doesn't exist, i.e. it has no being, etc.

B, iv, 999a26 (eighth problem): note the difference in the statements of this problem here and in the short list at 995b32-33. Here, ti para ta kath' hekasta; there, ti para tEn hulEn.

B, i and iv, 996a1-2 and 999b24-1000a4 (ninth problem): this is at first puzzling. What is meant? It has nothing to do with a, ii. The question is: are the unities of the [first] causes unities (1) of kind, or (2) of number? (1) If they are unities of kind, then they are not numerical unities, and there will be no knowledge of them (hen epi pantOn = hen epi pollOn). (2) But if they are numerical unities (alla mEn ei arithmOi hen) and each of the principles is one (kai mia hekastEn tOn arithmOn) there will be nothing beside the elements (ouk estai para ta stoicheia outhen heteron). Because unity in number is no different from individuality, so to speak (to gar arithmOi hen E to kath' hekaston legein diapherei outhen). Further elucidation is given by way of analogy to the elements of sound, in the middle of this passage, lines 28-32, kai mE hOsper...arithmOi hen eisin: they would be like the elements of sound. These being the same in kind differ in number. If they were not thus, but were one in number, there would be nothing else beside the elements. (Notice the confusion here of principles or causes, and elements.) That is to say, there would be no repetition of the original list, and no variety of them in words, etc.

What are at stake here are the competing claims of (1) eidetic unity (hen eidei) which allowed for repetition of elements of causes, but no knowledge, and (2) numerical unity (hen arithmOi), which yielded knowledge, but no repetition. Form (eidos) and number emphasize respectively mental and bodily aspects of whatever they are applied to. Formal unity indicates an abstract or conceptual unity of many things. Numerical unity indicates a concrete, physical or quasi-physical singleness. The "nature" and relation of those kinds of unity had not been thoroughly worked out, and they constituted the problem that is expressed here. Likewise the notions of principle and element, which are confused here in this problem (hoion tEsde tEs sullabEs...ouk estai para ta stoicheia outhen heteron), emphasize respectively mental and bodily aspects of the inquiry. "Element" has a bodily connotation and usage (and not just for us, but also for Aristotle) that "principle" does not have. The substitution of one for the other in this passage indicates a confusion in the writer's and possibly his readers' minds.

B, iv, 1001a4-b25 (eleventh problem): the structure of this passage may occasion some difficulty, and it raises a topic that had been briefly mentioned in the seventh problem, to te on kai to hen, which may still be strange to us. Here the problem is, are they substance (ousia), or not? To be sure that we understand precisely what is being said here, let us outline the passage:

A. Statement of the problem: are to hen kai to on (the One and Being) the substances of things (ousia tOn ontOn), and not different? Or are they some sort of substrate of another kind (1001a4-8)?

B. Some opinions (1001a8-19)

1. Plato and the Pythagoreans: substance (9-12)
2. the phusiologoi: various physical theories of the One and Being (love, fire, air, etc.) (12-19)

C. Discussion of the problem (1001a19-1001b6)

1. if they are *not* substance (ousia) (20-29)
   a. there are no other universals (21-24)
   b. if the One is not substance, there is no number separate from things (24-27)
2. if One and Being *are* some same thing

a. they must be substance, not something different
but the same (27-29)
b. but there is a big problem (a29-b6
1 how is there any multiplicity of beings? As
Parmenides said, everything is one (a31-b1)
2 again there is no number, whether one is not
or is substance (to hen ousia = ti auto hen)
(b1-6)
a if it is not, we showed why above (see
C. 1. b. above) (b3)
b if it is, there is the same problem as
with Being (i.e. the problem raised by
Parmenides): how will there be any other
one beside the One? It cannot be one (b3-6)
3 restatement: all things are one or many (b6)

Up to this point Aristotle has offered a dilemma that is complete in itself. Now the discussion takes a new turn suggested by the Parmenidean proposition (C. 2. B. 1 above) that everything is one and there is no multiplicity or division, eti ei adiaireton auto to hen, suggested both substantively and circumstantially. Zeno was very closely linked to Parmenides, as we know from Plato's dialogue. The first part of this new discussion is clearly related to what has preceded. It grows out of it quite naturally. But because the prior discussion is self-sufficient and this one brings in such new material (Zeno, etc.) the latter is placed under a separate major heading in this outline, for the sake of emphasis. The second part of it also seems to follow naturally as an additional consideration of traditional material in the shape of some current Platonic doctrine that was closely linked with all this.

D. New discussion

1. if the One is indivisible (as Parmenides had
suggested), then according to Zeno nothing
exists (b7-8)

a. Zeno's doctrine
   1 what, being added or taken away, makes not more or less, is not any being (b8-9)
   2 as being has bulk, and hence body (b10-11)
   3 other things sometimes make larger when added, sometimes not, like surface, line, point, monad (this argument of Zeno's was originally directed against the Pythagoreans, not against Parmenides, as might appear here, to refute their contention that points, etc. had bulk. It is here cited out of such a context by Aristotle.) (b11-13)

b. but Zeno argues coarsely and there can be something indivisible (b13-14). There is an answer to Zeno (b15). Such things as points, lines, etc., don't make larger when more are added, but how from such immaterial units or such additions will there be bulk? It is like saying the line is [made] of points (b15-19). (i.e. Zeno's mistake is to suggest that things must have bulk to exist.)

2. but if one supposes on the other hand [as Plato did] that number is produced by the One and the Other, one must no less inquire why and how sometimes number, sometimes bulk is produced, if the not-One is the Unequal (i.e. to mega kai to mikron, the dyad, matter). Because it is clear that bulk would not come to be somehow from the One and the Same, somehow from some number and the Same (b19-25).

Once more we must apologize for the awkwardness of our English. We are not just trying to translate. We are trying to determine whether we understand the Greek, and the reader is referred to the Greek.

There is here, we believe, a consistent and meaningful passage. It addresses questions that have already been raised before in the text, briefly. Attention has been called earlier to them (problem seven in B, iii, 998b22-27), and later a whole book, I, will be devoted to them. They are questions first about the nature of the One, or the notion of unity as we might put it, and its relations to Being and to their opposites, the Many and not-Being. These had been matters of perplexity for generations, when Aristotle was composing these lines. Parmenides, Zeno and Plato, referred to quite appropriately here, had been at the center of the controversies. It is impossible to understand these lines without understanding that context. The very language is inherited. Otherwise, as so often the case in Aristotle, it would seem silly.

The force of this tradition also explains why Aristotle's constructive metaphysics (Books E—Lambda) is divided into three ontologies instead of two. Two would answer his own original presuppositions: the structure of the four causes. His conceptual ontology of matter and form (E—Theta) and his quasi-physical ontology of the Unmoved Prime Mover and the Good (K—Lambda) are the two parts of his one science of the causes. The third ontology (Book I) is really an *ad hominem* excurse, a necessary response to one of the most prominent questions of his time, just as the final books (M, N) are appendices addressed to similar, not unrelated, but newer questions of number. These questions of unity, number, geometricals, rise appropriately to the surface here in this discussion of problems in Book B. Along with Plato's Idea theory they comprise the important underlying problems of the list, and they foreshadow the scope and structure of the treatise from E to N.

GAMMA
LANGUAGE AND METAPHYSICS

Book Gamma may be divided into two main parts. The first two chapters are concerned with the meanings of "being." The following, or last five chapters are concerned with the "axioms of knowledge," i.e. the famous laws of contradiction and of the excluded middle. The law of contradiction has a limited application in a metaphysics such as this, since it applies to subjects and attributes, whereas pure being, on hE on, the subject of this metaphysics, is without attributes. It is transcendent. Aside from pointing out this irony, we will have little to say about the last five chapters here. They contain no interpretive difficulties.

It is the first part that is difficult, especially chapter two. Chapter one briefly and simply points out *a* meaning of being, in fact the most important meaning for Aristotle's investigation here: being *qua* being, on hE on, pure being, abstract being (as we might call it). It is Plato's ontOs on and Parmenides' estin *redivivus*. It is of course the target of metaphysics.

Chapter two is devoted to the many meanings of being. To de on legetai pollachOs. In the course of arranging those meanings, this chapter makes use of a number of technical terms, which have been variously interpreted and which may be the cause of confusion. These terms are: synonym, homonym, pros hen, kath' hen, and so forth. The use and meaning here of some of them is different from their common use in English in our time, and that is far from helpful. Their use by and meaning for Aristotle may be found in many places aside from Gamma, ii, *Metaphysics*. The first chapter of Aristotle's *Categories*, and the commentary of Alexander Aphrodisias on the present chapter (*In Metaph. Arist.*, ed. Michael Hayduk, Berlin, 1891, p. 241) are most helpful. Ross' commentary, vol. I, p. 256-57 and 269 may also be consulted, as well as Bonitz, *Index*, and

Liddell, Scott, Jones. Using these references, we summarize the technical terms as follows:

Term	words	class or genus	root or derivation
synonym (= kath' hen)	same	same	not applicable
homonym	same	different	not applicable
paroym (= aph' henos kai pros hen)	different	different	same

For the sake of symmetry and completeness, we will add:

polynym	different	same	not applicable

Aristotle rarely uses such a term, and only then in a different context (*Historia animalium*, 489a2; *De mundo*, 401a12). Nevertheless, he seems to use it in such a manner, i.e. a different name for the same thing (eis On ho theos poluOnomos estin), even though Alexander Aphrodisias (280, 19) equates it with synonymy. It would fit here the situation of on and hen as different names for the same (ei de to on kai to hen tauton, etc.1003b23). See also Speusippus, fragment 32, ed. Lang.

The term, paronym, Aristotle does not use here, although he did use it in *Categories*, I, i. Paronyms differ in their flexion (case, gender, tense, etc.), but they "have an address to a name" (diapheronta tEi ptOsei tEn kata tounoma prosEgorian echei), i.e. a common root or derivation. Instead he uses the term pros hen, as our table above shows.

The main point is to distinguish (1) words that are different in meaning, but have some derivative (root) relationship to one another (paronyms), from (2) words that are different in meaning, but have no relation whatsoever (homonyms), and from (3) words that are different in meaning, but have a generic relationship to each other (synonyms). Alexander

Aphrodisias makes this quite clear (p. 241). Gamma, ii, has chiefly to do with the paronyms of "being" (ta aph' henos kai pros hen), but it has also to do with polynyms.

Before considering what Aristotle says in detail, let us look at the texts of Gamma, ii, and its paraphrase, Kappa, iii, as wholes, and ask ourselves, what is Aristotle trying to do in these two texts? It seems that in each case he is trying to do three things: (1) there are some theoretical comments, (2) there are some illustrative analogous examples, and (3) there are the many meanings of being, the pollachOs legetai to on-s, so to speak. Let us then inspect the texts in terms of these three activities:

(1) The theoretical comments. The many meanings of being are, in Gamma, ii:

pros hen kai mia tina phusin, to one and some one nature,
ouk homOnumos, not homonymously,
pros mian archEn, to one principle (or beginning),
kath' hen (dist. from pros hen) = synonymous,
pros mian phusin, to one nature,
kai tropon tina kath' hen (see above),
(ou gar ei pollachOs, heteras, all' ei mEte kath' hen mEte pros hen, see above)
(pros to prOton, to the first)

These are the phrases used wherever the question of meaning is raised by use of the word legetai or a paronym thereof. All but the last two are near the beginning of chapter ii of Gamma. The last two actually refer not to "being," but to other terms, and thus are parenthesized in the list above. So far these main points are made: (a) the meanings of being seem to point toward one primary meaning, nature or principle; (b) they are not homonymous; (c) they can have both a pros hen and a kath' hen relation to the one primary meaning (usually taken to mean homonymy and synnymy, with reference to Categories i, 1a for the meanings of these terms).

In K, iii:

> ei homonumOs ouk hupo mian epistEmEn, if homonymous, **not of** one science,
> ei kata ti koinon hupo mian epistEmEn, if with something in common, **of** one science,
> kath' hen ti kai koinon, after some one and common thing,

restate the main points (b., a., c. in that order) made above, excepting the mention of pros hen (which however is used plentifully in the examples to be studied below).

(2) The examples which Aristotle gives of multiplicity of meaning (pollachOs legesthai) are, in Gamma, ii:

> healthy, meaning protective of)
> healthy, meaning productive of)   health
> healthy, meaning signifying)   (pros hugieian)
> healthy, meaning receptive to)
> medical, meaning having)
> medical, meaning naturally suited for (pros))   medicine
> medical, meaning the work of)

In K, iii, they are:

> medical, referring to (pros) medicine
>   medical science, meaning knowledge of medicine
>   medical knife, meaning useful for medicine
> healthy, referring to (pros) health
>   healthy, meaning signifying health
>   healthy, meaning productive of health

The effect is the same in both chapters. The reference to one primary meaning, nature or principle (point (a) above) is made clear. The precise kind of linguistic relationship depends on the definitions of the linguistic relations. Since these can vary, even in Aristotle's own definitions and usages, it is not clear, and there is where much of the difference in interpretation seems to have lain. Thus little can be added with any certainty to points (b) and (c) in (1) above, i.e. whether these are homonyms or not, or paronyms, or synonyms, or pros hen equivocals, or something else. And perhaps little need be added. What we want to know is not Aristotle's linguistic theory of multiplicity *of meaning* here, but his theory of the multiplicity of *the meaning of being*, i.e., his linguistic theory of being. And we want to know this only to understand his theory of being itself. Let us now consider that theory:

(3) the many meanings of being (pollachOs legesthai to on) in Gamma, ii, are, in order of appearance:

> on hE on, being *qua* being,
> ousiai, substances,
> pathE ousias, properties or states of substance,
> hodos eis ousian, coming into being,
> phthorai, passings out of being,
> sterEsis , privation,
> poiotEtes , qualities
> poiEtika, productives,
> gennEtika ousias , generatives,
> ta pros tEn ousian legomena, things stated in relation to substance,
> onta, beings,
> ousia, substance,
> on, being,
> hen, one,
> tanantia, the contraries (several are named under this collective appellation);

n K, iii, in order of appearance,

pathos ontos hE on, property of being *qua* being,
hexis, state, or condition,
diathesis, disposition,
kinEsis, motion,
tanantia, the contraries,
ta sumbebEkota kath' hoson estin on, attributes (contingent or
necessary).

These lists hardly seem presented in a systematic fashion at first sight. Nevertheless they illuminate the multiplicity of the meanings of being, even if without any apparent order. It is not difficult to derive some order from them. Mind you, in doing so we are moving a step away from what is explicit in the texts, but I don't think we are moving very far away. Something like the following order seems capable of being derived easily, even though it may admit of some possible variation in detail:

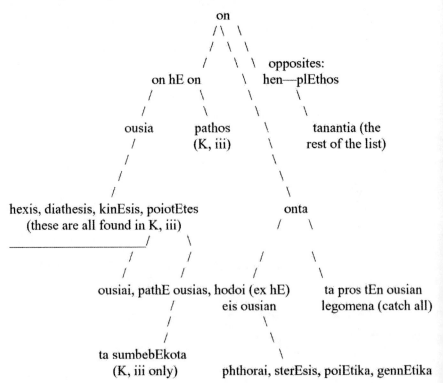

Even if it is possible to vary the details of this arrangement, the main features are apparent anyway. We use the word "being" first to denominate pure being, and individual beings; and Aristotle also investigated it in a special sense: the one. These are the three most general classes of meaning. Then there are the subdivisions of each of these, and subdivisions of the subdivisions, more or less as shown (not completely, to be sure). These are enough to indicate the many kinds of being, universal and individual, substantial and accidental, and others. Now it can be said with some clarity of meaning that our first science, the science we are seeking, deals with all being, but that means (1) pure being (on hE on), (2) being as one (hen) and its derivative contraries, and (3) individual beings, but only as being generally (onta hE onta), not as individuals. Thus it deals with being, its polynyms and paronyms.

This is in fact what the *Metaphysics* deals with in Books E—I. But it does so according to a different division of being, as we already know. Only the very initial division into on hE on and on ti bears any resemblance to the above. For a very simple reason: there (E—I) the investigation is ontological; here (Gamma, ii) it is linguistic. Gamma, ii, is still an introductory sort of investigation, putting us on our guard about our language, or giving us a taste of what is to come. Being means many things. There are many ways we speak of it, and it has many kinds itself. Here Aristotle only addresses the ways we speak of it; there the ways it is.

Gamma, ii, and K, iii, are also a response to the third and fifth problems of the list at the beginning of ü. "Since, speaking of being in many ways, we speak of all being [but] after one common [aspect], and in the same way of contraries, and those can all be subjects of one science, our problem is solved which we posed at the beginning; I mean the one[s] in which we asked how there could be one science of many and different kinds of being." Thus ends K, iii. "It is clear that it is [the task] of one science to investigate being *qua* being, and the subsistents in it *qua* being, and not only substances but subsistents of the kind mentioned and prior and posterior (i.e. the contraries?) and genus and species and whole and part and all other such things." Thus ends Gamma, ii.

Book Gamma plays an important part in the total scheme of the *Metaphysics*. Before launching into his main ontological investigation (E—I), Aristotle endeavors to clear up some difficulties that might stand in our way, that might arise from the varieties of the word, "being." If metaphysics deals with any being or all beings, it does so only in a qualified sense, which should by now be clear.

DELTA
SOME DEFINITIONS AND AMBIGUITIES

Whatever the origin of Book Delta, it occupies a significant place in the text of the whole *Metaphysics* as we now have that text. Consider this question: what is Delta? A sort of lexicon? This hardly seems likely. The "definitions" of archE, aition, stoicheion, phusis exhibit some confusion. hen is more thoroughly studied in Book I. The treatment of on is repeated in E, where it leads of course to the centerpiece of the whole treatise, the ontology of Eta thru Theta. Almost the same comment can be made about ousia. The most important and novel meaning of dunamis is not even mentioned; this is reserved for Theta. The explanation kolobon (chapter xxvii) is not even a catalogue of different meanings, like the others, but a list of the requirements of one meaning. And it is not too clear what role this term plays, anyhow. Perhaps more such deficiencies of a lexicon could be added.

How then should we regard Book Delta? Obviously it is devoted to a list, albeit not exhaustive, of the many meanings (pollachOs legesthai) of many terms. But to what end? If it is not trying to provide a comprehensive catalogue, it would seem plausible to infer that its purpose might be merely to alert the reader to the problem of ambiguity of most of the terms that must be used in this inquiry. Book Gamma has done this with reference to one term, being, to on. Delta does it for a number of terms. Neither book attempts to be complete or definitive. Both belong to the introductory, the propaedeutic part of the treatise. They perform similar and complementary functions. They serve to warn us of the difficulties of our task. Where the object of our search is ambiguous (Gamma) and the tools we use to conduct it are ambiguous (Delta), we may well be warned.

We might be warned, for example, of the danger of taking any proposition out of context, since often it is only the context that provides us with a clue, which of the many meanings of a term applies in a given instance. It is for this reason that structure and context have been emphasized here as possibly objective means of determining the meaning of the text.

Given this amorphous beginning, Aristotle seeks to find out what things are, and to give terms definite meaning within the scope of his "first science." But this may turn out to be impossible. Already among the many meanings of the many terms expounded in Delta, one may detect the persistent dichotomy. It receives no general notice, nor is it emphasized particularly, yet it is ever there. One wonders to what extent Aristotle was conscious of it. It is going to give us all trouble.

Here are some examples of it:

Chapter i, 1013a17, pasOn men oun koinon tOn archOn to prOton einai hothen E estin E gignetai E gignOsketai,

ii, 1013a24, aition legetai…ex hou…hoion to kalkos…allon de to eidos,

iii, 1014a32, ta tOn somatOn stoicheia legousin…paraplEsiOs de kai ta tOn diagrammatOn…kai tOn apodeixeiOn,

iv, 1015a7, phusis de hE te prOtE hulE…kai to eidos,

v, 1015a20, b6, anagkaion legetai hou aneu ouk endechetai zEn…hoion…hE trophE tOi zOiOi…eti hE apodeixeis tOn anagkaiOn,

vi, 1016a17, 32, hen legetai tOi to hupokeimenon tOi eidei einai adiaphoron, etc…eti de hen legetai hosOn to logos, etc.,

vii, 1017a22, 31, einai legetai hosaper sEmainei ta schEmata tEs katEgorias …einai sEmainei kai to estin hoti alEthes,

viii, 1017b10, 21, ousia legetai ta te hapla sOmata…eti to ti En einai, ix, 1018a6, 10, hOn hE hulE mia E eidei E arithmOi tauta legetai kai hOn hE   ousia mia...hetera de legetai hOn E ta eidE pleiO E hulE E ho logos tEs ousias,

x, 1018a20, antikeimena legetai antiphasis...kai eis ha ta eschata hai genesis kai phthorai,

xi,1018b12, 30, protera kai hustera legetai...kata topon...kata chronon...kata kinEsin, etc....allon de tropon to tEi gnOsei proteron,.

xii,1019a15, dunamis legetai hE men archE kinEseOs E metabolEs E en heterOi H hEi heteron, hoion E hE oikodomikE dunamis estin...The other meaning of dunamis is conspicuously absent in this chapter. Were it present, it would fit in with the above contrasts.

Let these suffice, although more examples may be found at 1021a29, 1022a9-10, 1021a21, 1022b1-2, 1023b12-17, 238 1024b4, 1024b26, and possibly elsewhere.

None of these taken separately might be the cause for much comment, but taken all together they assume a new significance. There is running through all of Book Delta, or nearly all of it, this persistent dichotomy: nearly every term is applicable and is applied to both the material and the noetic aspects of our experience. Not just the central terms, like being and substance, which are the objects of this first science, but also the terms used to approach those, the primary ones like cause, element, nature, and the secondary ones like same, opposite, and so forth, exhibit this dichotomy. Thinking back, we may recall that this echoes the message of Gamma, the primary distinction of on hE on and ousia except with the addition of the traditional special case of unity, a legacy eventually rejected. It also reflects a dichotomy at the beginning of Book A in Aristotle's scheme of causation. Matter and form themselves show this contradiction. Both have material and abstract meanings. So to a less obvious extent do the moving and final causes. All these reflect the key problem of the *Metaphysics*.

E, I
"WHAT KIND OF SCIENCE DO WE SEEK?"

Following in line the introduction (A, i) and the discussions of causes, and their prior recognition and finiteness (A, ii—ix; a), of problems (B), of linguistic and logical considerations (Gamma), and of definitions (Delta), the first chapter of Book E closes in on the title topic: its chief function is to ask, what kind of a science is the science we are seeking? It narrows the scope of the inquiry.

To accomplish this, it does three things.

First it discusses kinds of being: on hE on and on ti (being *qua* being and particular being[s], 1025b3-18). This section is not simply a repetition of Gamma, i—ii, much as it may seem like it on account of the repetition of the subject terms. There the viewpoint is linguistic; here, not. It is rather directed to the "thing" being signified, not to the words; to the *res*, not the *vox*. It is ontological. We are now discussing being, its two chief kinds: on hE on and on ti (= onta).

Second, it discusses kinds of sciences: practical, productive and theoretical; and of the theoretical: physics, mathematics and our first science. The last is for Aristotle here "theology." For us it is metaphysics (1025b9-1026a23). Aristotle concludes this part by ranking these. (Also, an important, very brief remark, 1026a9, forshadows M, iii.)

The third and concluding section of this chapter, 1026a23-32, addresses the question: what kind of a science are we seeking? It is the most important of all. It has two parts:

1. It asks first whether our first science is of a universal (or the universal), or about some one kind and nature (phusin), in the lines 1026a23-27. We may ask whether this distinction is the same one which we will have occasion to

point out later, and which distinguishes Books Z—Theta from Book Lambda, i.e. the distinction of an internal, abstract, separate and motionless being from an external, Unmoved Prime Mover (about which more later). Such a foreshadowing is quite possible, but not at all certain. It is also possible that Aristotle is simply distinguishing the universal on hE on as the object of the first science, from physical things, onta or on ti, since this is the purport of the immediately following lines:

2. "If on the one hand there is no substance other than those in physical things, our first science is physics; but if on the other hand there is some motionless [i.e. separate] substance, it is prior, and philosophy [i.e. our first science] is first, and it is of a universal [or the universal], and of being *qua* being, of what is and its properties" (1026a27-32).

These lines are of importance in fixing the scope of the inquiry as the investigation of on hE on.

From this point on, Aristotle proceeds in E, ii, to subdivide being *qua* being itself, and to narrow down the inquiry even further. E, i, is the end of the introductory part of the *Metaphysics*. It brings us to the target, so to speak, of the "science we seek."

E—THETA
WHAT IS BEING?

The core of the *Metaphysics* must be for us the four books, E, Z, Eta and Theta. They comprise the first and the most important of the three ontologies that follow the propaedeutic books, and that are followed in turn by the two appendices on number (M, N). The other two ontologies are a traditional one in I, which Aristotle rejects; and one conceived in terms of motion, in K and Lambda, which he does not reject. Nevertheless the latter is probably an earlier effort, and it is certainly less significant for us. E-Theta deal directly and explicitly with the question, what is being? They do so in a sense of the word "metaphysics" that has accrued to it over the ages, "beyond the physical," i.e. non-physical.

Being, as is well known by now, means to Aristotle many things. The list of these provides the organization of the central books, E—Theta. E, ii, gives the summary list of four: (1) accidental being, (2) being as truth, (3) the categories, and (4) potentiality and actuality. E, ii—iii, eliminate accidental being from further consideration. E, iv, and (curiously out of place) Theta, x, eliminate being as truth. Z and Eta are addressed to being of the categories, or, as it turns out, just one of the categories, the first, ousia, substance. Theta, i—ix, deal with being as potentiality and actuality. Thus the core of the inquiry of the *Metaphysics*, the question, what is being? may now be reduced to the three books, Z, Eta and Theta, and two questions: what is ousia, and what are potentiality and actuality?

It turns out that Aristotle declines to answer one of these two questions, i.e. what potentiality and actuality *are*. Furthermore, not only does he fail to give a definition but he explicitly says that there are things that cannot be defined. These are clearly among them. Such things belong to the assumptions of a science, as he makes out in the *Posterior Analytics*. One can only give examples, as he does in the present case. The examples are good ones, in so far as we all immediately share (I believe it is safe to say) his intuition. Potentiality and actuality are self-evident concepts based upon the experience of all of us. So Book Theta is devoted mainly, after elimination of other, common meanings of potency (which are not our concern) and a brief discussion of the Megarian doctrine, to the various things that can be said about potentiality and actuality, but there is no effort to define what these *are*.

Such is not the case with the remaining kind of being: ousia. Books Z and Eta are the effort to determine what ousia is. Here there is no such disclaimer as is found in Theta, vi: ou dei pantos horon zEtein. Examples here will not suffice. These two books attempt to give an account (logos) of ousia. They attempt to answer the question, what is being? They constitute the innermost core of the *Metaphysics*.

Although they are confusing at first, a review of Z and Eta at large reveals a structure that makes sense. There are two ways to give an account of, or to define anything:

(1) we can tell what its components are,
(2) we can identify it by differentiation from other
    individuals in a class or species, and (if asked)
    further differentiate that encompassing class from
    other classes, and so on, until we reach some final
    or primary set (for Aristotle, his ten or eight
    etc. categories, as listed in *Categories*, iv, or
    in *Metaphysics*, 1027a25, etc.).

Let us, for brevity's sake, call the first kind of account a "componential" account; the second kind, a "differential" account. The second might also be called a "classificatory" account, since class and difference go hand in hand here. All of us use both of these ways sufficiently frequently that a little reflection should provide many examples, and establish their validity.

Aristotle uses both methods in Z and Eta. Furthermore he switches back and forth intermittently from one to the other, sometimes suddenly and with little or no formal announcement, and this may be a source of confusion in these two books. For example, in Z, iii—xi, he seems to be talking componentially for the most part, although problems of differentiation impinge in chapters iv, v and vi. But in Z, xii—xvi, he is talking of classes and differences. In the latter part of xvii we find him dealing componentially again; in Eta, i, componentially (reflecting the early part of Z); in Eta, ii, differentially, yet ending with an explicit acknowledgement of the two kinds of account (1043a19-21). Z, iii—vi is quite mixed.

One can easily be confused by these alternations. It is necessary to sort them out, and to see clearly these two different approaches to ousia. To inquire into their *raison d'être* may reveal to us something about the nature of our search and its object. Why does Aristotle vaccilate between them? They are reflected in the four things that ousia is said to be, at the beginning of Z, iii: to ti En einai and hupokeimenon belong to the (1) componential account, while katholou and genos are part of the (2) differential account. Why this dichotomy?

Furthermore these two ways are themselves subject to a peculiar characteristic, and this characteristic creates an additional problem: together they represent a dichotomy; separately each leads again to a dichotomy. In all cases it is the same dichotomy replicating itself:

A. Together:

The componential account (1) is analagous to a material ccount. The notion of components bears a very strong affinity to the notion of elemental materials. Meanwhile the differential account (2) is analagous to an intellectual or mental production. It results in nothing of a material nature, but in a final difference, the mental analysis. Even the individual identified by the last *differentia* tends to vanish from materiality, as all factors common with other individuals have been set aside.

B. Separately:

1. First the componential account: the products of this are matter and form. Matter is componential. Form is identified differentially. Thus the original dichotomy is replicated on its componential side. Carried a step further, each of these is replicated again: a. matter as matter is easily perceived, but Aristotle's hulE noEtE is a conception of the other kind; b. form as form is properly understood, but we all continually succumb to the temptation to materialize this conception. Furthermore, there is a material meaning of form.

2. Second, the differential account: the products of this account are class and difference, and the individual discovered by the final difference. Class and difference are mental. But the individual is not We usually perceive the individual as a very palpable thing. In Aristotle's system ta kath' hekasta are the things of this world; if they were anywhere else, they would be Plato's Ideas (as Aristotle sees those: tinas phuseis para tas en tOi ouranOi—997b6). Carried a step further, there have been realists (in the technical sense) who succumbed to the temptation of attributing the same sort of reality to classes that is attributed individuals; and on the other hand we have just seen how to strip individuals of materiality, stripping them of all their properties by progressive differentiation.

As far as we can pursue this we find the original dichotomy replicated at every turn. We seem to be held in the grip of the original dichotomy: ousia is something we perceive and something we conceive. We can approach it from either direction. It is palpable things; it is a conception.

It should be no surprise that Aristotle was entangled, or that we are. The nature of his entanglement explains some of the difficulty of his text for the reader. Not only is he caught by these ramifications of the dichotomy that keep popping up, but with his never-failing inquisitiveness he keeps turning from one to the other in pursuit of them. This is what makes Books Z and Eta so difficult to organize. Perhaps some understanding of the underlying difficulty sketched here will help us through these twists and turns as we pursue with Aristotle the nature of ousia.

Aristotle's hylomorphism (matter and form) is a step beyond Plato's Form theory, as an ontology. It reveals the dual nature not of the world as a whole, but of each this-thing in it. All this has been very useful. But he carried Plato's difficulty right along with him in his own baggage. His form, like Plato's Forms, is utterly separate from his matter, if in a different way. Yet at the same time his form can be materialized, in the fashion of 997b5-12 or otherwise. And his matter is both sensible and intelligible. Each of his two concepts may take on some of the color of the other. The history of thought shows that this actually happened. At every level reality is analyzable into form and matter. As for Aristotle, we have learned how he altered Plato's doctrine at the same time that he remained a Platonist. He was caught in the same dichotomies as Plato.

E, II—Z, I
KINDS OF BEING

After establishing that on haplOs, or on hE on, is the object of our inquiry, Aristotle in these chapters narrows down the target, thus:

on haplos = 1. accidental being, eliminated,   E. ii—iii,

          2. truth, eliminated,   E, iv; Theta, x,

          3. potentiality and actuality,   Theta, i—ix,

          4. categories = a. quality,

                  b. quantity, etc., all

                  eliminated, except ousia,   Z, i.

This is a brief scheme of the progress of these four chapters. What are we to make of it?

1. It exhibits a certain unity in this transition from the introductory books to the core of the treatise.

2. It exhibits some similarities to the breakdown of the meanings of being in Book Gamma, in which several (although not all) of the same names of kinds of being appear. But there the scheme was an expanding one. Here it is a contracting one. That is, there the aim seemed to be to develop the varieties of (the meanings) of being; here, to eliminate them, to find the one which is to be the concern of our first science. There the treatment was linguistic and propaedeutic; here we are launched upon the ontology proper.

3. This scheme terminates with ousia. Being as potentiality and actuality will be treated somewhat perfunctorily (as an assumption) in Book Theta. Our first ontology will concentrate on ousia. Ousia is the "tighter" concept substituted for on haplOs or on hE on, just as this in turn had been silently substituted by Aristotle for Plato's ontOs on, and that in turn for Parmenides' estin. There is on the one hand a continuity in these terms,

while there is on the other a progressive development. Ousia, as a target of the forthcoming ontology, is a refinement of the same old target, a closer definition (looking at it from outside, as it were) of the sort of being that Aristotle is seeking. It is not something different from on or estin. It is rather a precision of those terms. Its difference lies in what it eliminates.

4. The translations, substance, *substantia*, are deceiving. The connotations of these are of something palpable. ousia, like on, is an abstraction, at the same time that it is palpable. This is precisely the problem that will be faced in the forthcoming ontology of ousia in Books Z and Eta. In all the effort to eliminate ambiguity and to attain precision, this dichotomy will never be eliminated. This is not without the highest significance, since ousia is one of the main objects of inquiry of the *Metaphysics*. The immediately forthcoming ontology in Z and Eta, the ontology of the two causes, matter and form, will be the study of ousia. What is ousia?

5. The same problem is raised by the equivalence in the text: ousia = ti esti (Z, i; Delta, vii). The latter phrase also gives ousia an appearance of palpability, "thingness," concreteness, individuality. Ti esti seems much closer to on ti and onta, beings, things, individuals, than to on haplOs, pure being, being itself (even though Aristotle explicitly distinguishes to on from ousia in 1028a30-31). Up to this point in the *Metaphysics*, however, we do not know what ousia or ti estin are. It is the purpose of what follows to determine just that.

On haplOs and ousia are also there (1028a30) called to prOtos on. Immediately thereafter four meanings of prOton are given for this context. They include a mental primacy, seeming to indicate that these are abstractions or conceptions. What is ousia?

Z III—XVII
THE INVESTIGATION OF OUSIA

Someone reading Book Z chapter by chapter might find it confusing. It might help dispel this confusion to begin with a brief outline of this part of the text:

The whole appears at first to reflect the initial summary statement in chapter iii, but there are amendments to the scheme that appear to closer inspection later in the book. One sees in the later chapters that the genus and the universal are treated more or less as equivalent to one another. The conjunction may not always be exact (as Bonitz notes in his *Index*, p. 150, 356) from an outside point of view, but they are treated conjointly in chapters xii—xvi. This vacates the fourth position in the fourfold scheme that Aristotle began with, but the vacancy is filled in the opening lines of the thirteenth chapter (1038b1-3) where in place of to genos there is substituted to ek toutOn (i.e. ek tou hupokeimenou kai tou ti En einai). The seventeenth and last chapter of the book fulfills this revised scheme, as the overall outline shows.

Also there is a discussion in the middle of the book, chapters vii—xi, which at first looks like a departure from the fourfold scheme of the rest of the book. As a matter of fact, prominent modern scholars, led by Natorp and Ross (see Ross, vol. II, p. 181, 204), reject these chapters as an "interruption." Not so. Not so at all. The discussion of ta gignomena is a very proper subdivision of the discussion of ousia, hinted at in chapter iii, 1029a34-35, and repeated in Book Eta. Furthermore the structure of this special discussion parallels the structure of the encompassing whole. It is based on matter and form, and in the simplest terms.

to hupokeimenon : to ti En einai :: matter : form

This mathematical (in appearance) proportion is little more than a metaphor to show that substrate and essence are each respectively synonymous with matter and form. In fact Aristotle is sometimes quite explicit about this. References are collected by Bonitz in his *Index*, p. 219, 474, 764, 785, and 798.

The classification of the three kinds of ta gignomena in chapters vii and ix does not seem the most necessary contribution to the discussion, and may account for some of our confusion here. It is the substrate-essence and matter-form couplets that lead us to the heart of this discussion, which is in turn the heart of Aristotle's metaphysics of being and ousia, or at least of one of its two main phases. This inquiry in Book Z is centered upon this pair of pairs of paired concepts:

1. a component pair

   a. hupokeimenon—hulE (substrate—matter)
   b. to ti En einai—eidos (morphE) (essence—form)

2. a differentiating pair

   a. katholou—genos (universal—class)
   b. To kath' hekaston—diaphora (individual—difference)

Furthermore the first (component) pair combined produce what Aristotle refers to as to sunolon or to ek toutOn; the second (differentiating) pair, to ti. These are nearly synonymous. But the main point is that at all levels, even at the lowest level of the synonyms, such as substrate and matter, there is a dichotomy, and it is the same dichotomy, for which we will choose from among the many possible equivalent terms: matter and form. These two approaches (1. and 2.) reflect it, as Aristotle himself notes,

1043a19-21. Within each of these two approaches, the dichotomies (a. and b.) reflect it. One of them even supplies our chosen terms for it, while in the other

katholou, genos : to kath' hekaston, diaphora :: matter : form

This latter proportion is made clear among other places in Delta, xxviii, 1024b3-4, 8-9). The pairs of synonyms reflect it. hupokeimenon, substrate, tends to be found in more abstract, that is formal, contexts; hulE, matter, in more concrete, material contexts. The other pairs similarly. Finally even single terms exhibit the dichotomy. There are two kinds each of matter and of form. There are the morphE hupokeimenE of 1029a3 (Aristotle does not actually use this term, but it labels aptly what he is talking about there), and the hule noEtE (a term he does use) of 1037a5.

All these couplets correspond to a division within the human observer himself. Matter and form (and their correlates) are apprehended in the first instance by the senses and the intellect respectively (although this too is reversible). We are divided.

All of them, matter and form, class and difference, substrate and essence, body and mind..., all are distinct and separate, and at the same time they are connected and convertible. Their separateness and distinctness and otherness are typified most notably in the discovery in chapter x that after all matter itself is unknowable, hE d' hulE agnOstos kath' hautEn (1036a8). Their inseparability and their mutual ties are typified in the famous concept of hulE noEtE in chapter xi. It is this simultaneous separateness and connectedness that is the discovery of Book Z for us. Aristotle does not explicitly draw such a generalization. It is a good question, whether he thoroughly understood it. Nevertheless the facts are there and the implications not hard to see. Being itself transcends Aristotle's law of contradiction (Gamma, iii). It is beyond all predicates, beyond all attributes, beyond all properties (Z, iv, v). It is a web of contradictions.

There is much precedent for neoplatonic transcendentalism in Z, *Metaphysics*.

To summarize some of the main points that Book Z teaches us about ousia:

1. it is form, matter and their combination,
2. in a sense it cannot be matter by itself,
3. in a sense it seems to be form,
4. but form by itself has no attributes or properties; is utterly transcendent,
5. and matter by itself is unknowable,
6. substrate and essence are synonyms for matter and form respectively, employed in relatively formal as opposed to material contexts,
7. yet all these pairs are bound together actually, however much they may be distinguished intellectually,
8. and all of them can be subdivided into material and formal senses,
9. and the entire process of defining ousia by such components is paralleled by another process using division and difference,
10. and these two larger processes are related to each other as matter to form,
11. and all of this reflects a parallel dichotomy in ourselves.

Even more concisely summarized, Book Z reveals

1. the dual nature of ousia,
2. the unaccountability of matter and the transcendence of form,
3. and the similarity of the human situation.

There are two kinds of questions regarding the detailed elucidation of Z iii—xvii. One has to do with the plain relevance of some passages with the central theme of the investigation. The other has to do with an apparent confusion of the discussions of matter and form and the discussions of definition and division (genus and difference). These two kinds of interruptions in the smooth flow of the discussion are the causes of most of the difficulties in the text. Each has been mentioned before, and it is of utmost importance that we identify the lines of cleavage, if we are to explain the interruptions and difficulties. Therefore a detailed organization of the text of Z, iii—xvii, chapter by chapter, will now be undertaken. The reader may check this outline against the text, for his own satisfaction. Thus he has the means to test the cogency of much of the above argument, and possibly make improvements.

DETAILED OUTLINE OF Z, iii—xvii

iii

A. Summary statement: ousia =   1028b33-36

    to ti En einai
    to katholou
    to genos
    to hupokeimenon

B. Ousia = to hupokeimenon   b36-1029a2

C. to hupokeimenon is   1029a2

    1. hE hulE, adunaton de, matter? impossible   a2-27
    2. to ex amphoin, apheteon? dismiss it   a27-32

1. they are excluded, except secondarily   b16-28
2. also their inclusion in definition   b28-a1
   causes confusion and reduplication
3. recap   1031a1-11

C. Summary recap of iv,   v a11-14

vi

A. To ti En einai (= ousia) = hekaston, it seems   a15-18

B. In the case of accidents and properties, it   a19-28
   seems *not* (tOn legomenOn kata sumbebEkos)

C. tOn kath' hauta legomenOn tauto;   a28-31

   1. if separate, they'd be like Platonic Ideas   a31-b3
   2. if detached from each other (i.e. the
      individual and its essence), what we know
      and what is would be different   b3-10
   3. the essence of the good cannot be in   b11
      anything but the good
   4. and so they must be one and the same   b14-18
      (more so if they were Forms)
   5. recap   b18-28

D. Some additional comments   b28-a4

E. Recap   1032a4-6

F. The sophistical objections are met in the same   a6-10
   way as the objection to "Socrates = the essence
   of Socrates" (an individual). (As Ross points
   out in his footnote to this, Aristotle has been
   discussing an individual *universal.*)

vii

viii

ix

C. Recap: neither matter nor form nor ousia nor   b7-19
   nor any of the other categories come into
   being; they all pre-exist

X

A. Ought an account of the parts (of ousia)   1034b22-24
   be contained in the account of the whole?

  1. every account has parts (note confusion: a part b20
     of the account is an account of the parts)
  2. examples   b24-28
  3. quantitative parts eliminated from   b28-34
     consideration

B. Let us examine the parts of ousia   b34

  1. they are matter and form and to d' ek toutOn   1035a1-2
  2. ways in which matter is and is not a   a2-4
     part (it is not a part of abstractions)
     a. examples   a4-22
     b. recap   a22-25
     c. more examples   a25- b3

  3. priority and posteriority of parts   b3-27
     a. parts of an account are prior   b3-1 1
     b. parts of matter are posterior   b11-14
     c. parts of living beings are and   b14-27
         are not prior

  4. universals and individuals: ousia is   b27-31
     not a universal, but a sunolon ti

C. Recap   b31-1036a25

1. the parts: form, matter, to sunolon   b31-33
2. the parts of the account are only of the form   b33-34
   alla tou logou merE ta tou eidous monon estin
   a. an account is only of the universal   b34-a1
      1 a circle or a soul = its essence   1036a1-2
      2 this circle (combined matter and form)   a2-8
          is the object of sensation or direct
          knowledge (E aisthEtou E noEtou) not
          of definition (= logos, account)
   b. matter itself is unknowable,   a8-13
      hE d' hulE agnOstos kath' hautEn
3. priority and posteriority are not simple or   a13-25
   absolute (this is somewhat opaque and beside
   the main point. However, see Tredennick's
   translation, Loeb ed., I, 363; it is as good
   an explanation as any.)

xi

A. When is a part part of the form? When is it   1036a26-27
   part of a combined (tou sunolou)

   1. this is necessary to know for definition   a27-31
      (which is of essence and form)
   2. some examples
      a. in a bronze, stone or wooden circle   a31-34
         (combined) the material is not part
         of the ousia of the circle (form)
      b. if all circles were bronze, one might   a34-b3
         think the bronze were part of the
         ousia of the circle
      c. the flesh and bones of a man, are   b3-7
         part of his form, or not?

xii

2. arguments *pro* b16-23,a14-21
    a. does it inhere, not as an essence,   1038b16-23
    but like a genus? Clearly, there
    is an account of it
    b. if it is not a universal, there is   1039a14-21
    no account of or definition of ousia
3. *or* there is, in a sense, and there is   a21-23
    not, in another sense. This will be
    clarified later (is it?)

xiv

A. What happens when you juxtapose the (Platonic)   a24-26
   Idea theory and the theory of genus and
   difference (they are incompatible)
B. Forms and genera, although logically the same,   a26-30
   are either one in number, i.e. the same, or
   they are different

   1. if one in number, or the same   a30-b6
     a. if there is a separate absolute man, there   a30-b2
       must also be separate absolute higher genera,
       like animal, two-footed. Are they all one?
     b. again   b2-6
       1 participation in two-footedness and many-
         footedness is impossible; these are opposites
       2 if man doesn't participate thus, what sense
         calling an animal footed or two-footed?
   2. if other, or different   b7-17
     a. they will be infinite in number   b7-9
     b. absolute animal will be many, etc.   b9-14
     c. from what does a particular animal come?   b14-16

d. the difficulties are greater with   b16-17
   sensible individuals
3. if these alternatives are impossible,   b17-19
   clearly there are no [Platonic] Forms

XV

A. Ousia = 1. a combined, to sunolon   1039b20-22
           2. a definition, ho logos

B. The combined is perishable; the definition is not   b22-27

C. Of individual sensibles there is no definition   b27-a4

1. statement   b27-a1
2. demonstration: no necessity attaches to them

D. Nor is there any definition of Platonic Ideas   1040a8-b4

1. Ideas are individual; definition uses   a8-14
   common general terms
2. rebuttal of the objection that they can   a14-b4
   be both common and individual
   a. two-footed animal is predicable of   a15-21
      both two-footed and animal
   b. what are prior in being cannot be   a21-22
      abolished together
   c. elements of ideas
      1 if there are such, they are predicable   a22-25
         of many
      2 if there are not, there is no knowledge   a25-27
   3. eternal beings (e.g. the sun, moon) cannot   a27-b2
      be defined
   4. why doesn't one [of the Platonists] produce   b2-4
      a definition of an Idea?

xvi

A. It is clear that of apparent substances most are potentialities: parts of animals, earth, fire, air have no unity, ouden hen estin, all' hoion sOros	1040b5-16
B. To hen kai to on are not and are the ousia of things	b16-27
1. they are not	b16-21
2. they are more ousia than elements, etc. are; and these are not at all, if ousia is not	b21-23
a. ousia belongs to nothing but itself	b23-24
b. nor does to hen belong to more than one	b25-26
3. no universal exists in other than the individual	b26-27
C. The Platonists are both right and wrong in separating Forms	b27-a3
1. they are right if the Forms are substances	b28-29
2. they are wrong in calling Form an Idea (universal?), hen epi pollOn	b29-30
a. the reason is they cannot explain what such separate imperishable substances are, other than individual sensibles	b30-32
b. they just make them the same in form as the perishables, and add "auto-" [cf. 997b5-12]	b32-34
c. yet eternal substances must be admitted that we do not see or don't know what they are	b34-a3
D. Recap: there is no ousia from universals or from [other] ousia	1041a3-5

xvii

    c. it is made of elements, is not an element   b19-22
      itself
    d. of not one but many   b22-25
  2. it is something not elemental, and the cause   b25-28
    of its being *this* is its ousia.

Z is not an easy book. This outline is not intended to substitute for, or translate the text, but to help us return to it, and penetrate it, keeping the forest in view, while looking at the trees.

ETA
A RECAPITULATION

An outline of Book H will look something like this:

I. Two classes of ousia   i

    A. Those everyone agrees on: physicals
    B. Individual theories

II. Other considerations

    A. Parts of definition of ousia need to be examined
    B. Universal and genus eliminated

III. The agreed on class: the sensibles

    A. Ousia is
        1. matter, hE hulE
        2. form, hE morphE (kai ho logos)
        3. the combination, to ek toutOn
    B. Ousia as matter
        1. statement
        2. reasons
    C. Ousia as actuality   ii
        1. what is ousia actually?
        2. difference
        3. analogy of ousia to difference
        4. examples
        5. componential and differential accounts compared
        6. recap: the three constituents of ousia (as in A. above)

Even a cursory glance at this outline reveals several characteristics of H that are similar to Z, and that indicate that the two books are mutually confirming. H uses the concepts, to hupokeimenon, to ti En einai, to genos, to katholou, used by Z, and also matter (hulE) and form (morphE). Like Z, H drops universal and genus. The examination of sensibles, which occupies a prominent place in H, is the equivalent of the inquiry into ta gignomena in Z, vi—xi. Both inquiries produce the same hylemorphic doctrine. This seems to confirm our opinion that Z, vi—xi, is not an "interruption" in the sense of being an extraneous element.

An examination of the parts of the account of ousia was a prominent feature of Z (chapter x). The same is explicitly recommended in H, i, 1042a18-21, although it is not carried out so extensively. Also notice in H the alternation between what have been termed the componential and differential accounts. What is more, in H, ii, there is an explicit reference to these two kinds of account: eoike gar ho men dia tOn diaphorOn logos tou eidous kai tEs energeias einai, ho d' ek tOn enuparchontOn tEs hulEs mallon (1043a19-21).

Finally there seems to be some sort of similarity between H, ii, iii and vi and Z, xii—xvi, in that definition and difference play a prominent part in both. Yet what are the parts that they play? This is more difficult to say. Does H help to explain Z in these parallel chapters?

This brings us to the other side of the comparison of the two books, to the differences between them. H has some distinct new departures. One is the much greater emphasis given to matter and form, on the whole, than to substrate and essence. But most noticeable is the introduction of the pair of concepts, potentiality and actuality, as a new dimension of matter (substrate) and form (essence). For this is just what this new pair is. Chapter ii commences: epei d' hE men hOs hupokeimenE kai hOs hulE ousia homolegetai, autE d' estin hE dunamei...(1042b9-10), and ends: hE d' hOs morphE kai energeia...(1043a27-28). Along the way, phaneron dE ek toutOn hoti hE energeia allE allEs hulEs kai ho logos (1043a12-13). Later passages in chapters iii (1043a37-b4) and vi (1045a30-33) reconfirm this equivalence.

Matter = potentiality. Form = actuality.

This deserves inspection. There is much more to it than these simple formulas. We have already seen the ambiguity of, say, matter: hulE aisthEtE and hulE noEtE. We may expect something like that here. Regardless of its association with matter in Aristotle's hylemorphic theory, potentiality is also an idea, a product of the mind, identifiable by or in the mind. The world of bodies and sensation is the actual world, unless you are a complete mystic. It may be that the *real* world consists of both, actual and potential, if by the "actual" and the "real" we mean something different.

These linkages, of potential with the mental (Aristotle had implied this before in his solution of Zeno's paradoxes, in *Physics*, VIII) and of potential with matter (no more a contradiction than the hulE noEtE) add quite a new dimension to the doctrine of the *Metaphysics*. It is true that ousia is found by Aristotle in the individual (to kath' hekaston), and in form as the component of the combination that gives it its individuality and this-ness, but this is true only in actuality. That is not the whole story. Potentially it is not true at all. Potentially ousia is either or both matter or/and form, and is not a "this" or an individual. Furthermore it is also an abstraction, being by itself (being as truth, and accidental being set aside), on hE on, or at any rate its equivalent. What is the status of this potentiality? Has Aristotle introduced it for nothing? If so, then abstraction is nothing, and the mind is nothing. Then of course the question becomes, what do we mean by nothing? and we are back in the grip of the old and original dichotomy. And we can ask also, do we think that our thoughts do not exist—somehow?

If it was not for nothing that the concept of potentiality was introduced here, and if we seek to know what substance (ousia) and being (on) are potentially as well as actually, abstract as well as concrete, then the usual and the scholastic understanding of Aristotle's *Metaphysics* is insufficient, and Parmenides and Plato were not on a wild goose chase in their search for estin and ontOs on. These were abstractions and potentialities, whatever names those thinkers had (or didn't have) for them. Whatever the historical relationship of Z and H is (and I will leave that for others to discuss), it seems clear that these two books are complementary. They cover enough common ground to confirm one another, while each contributes something of its very own: Z, the unknowability of matter and the transcendence of form; H, the concepts of potentiality and actuality.

THETA
POTENTIALITY AND ACTUALITY

Having introduced in his ontology of matter and form in Book H a new pair of concepts, potentiality and actuality (these parallel matter and form and assist our understanding of them), it is appropriate that Aristotle next addresses himself directly to these two new concepts. That is just what he does in Book Theta.

It seems clear from the tenor of Theta that Aristotle does not draw the conclusions which we have drawn above in the discussion of Eta, about the significance of potentiality. Thus we are forced to distinguish between (1) what appear to us to be the compelling implications of Aristotle's text (potentiality, recognized by the mind, thus a mental existent, is deserving of inquiry in its own right), and (2) his explicit doctrine (something more limited).

The first part of Theta, chapters i and ii, is largely devoted to the common meaning of dunamis: this is what we usually call "power," the physical force that makes things move. This is followed in chapters iii—v by a discussion of a question, said to have been raised by the Megarians: does power only exist when it is acting (or active)? This may easily be transformed into the questions: is there any other kind of "power" (dunamis)? Is there a "power" that exists, let us say, in a quiescent state? At first this seems like a contradiction in terms, especially if you forget or put out of your mind such modern, sophisticated terms as "potential energy," but it is just the purpose of this chapter to suggest that there is such a novel sort of power. The Megarian discussion is a foil for introducing this.

For this new sort we usually use the word, "potentiality," to distinguish it from "power." Aristotle often distinguishes it by the use of the dative, dunamei, as opposed to dunamis. Likewise we often make a parallel distinction between "activity" (and perhaps "action") and "actuality," whereas Aristotle himself in this instance uses his terms more indistinctly (Bonitz, *Index*, p. 251). But does he see that here the dichotomies are reproducing themselves in the same way that they did in form and matter?

Aristotle directly addresses the nature of this new potentiality in chapter vi. And what happens? He does not attempt to define it. In fact he emphatically states that not everything needs to be defined. Examples will do. And he gives them, adequately. In short it looks as though we have some sort of an assumption here. The two chapters, vi and vii, are given over to additional discussion: that potentiality and actuality are correlatives, kinds of potentiality (haplOs, gnOsei), potentiality and matter, etc.

Chapter viii is the second climax of the book. Chapter viii declares the priority of actuality, and gives the reasons therefore. It is the explicit basis of Aristotle's belief in the priority of form and the individual as ousia. If actuality is prior to potentiality, then it seems to follow that ousia in its actual mode is prior to ousia in its potential mode.

Aristotle's arguments for the priority of actuality, in chapter viii, are addressed to priority (1) logOi, (2) chronOi, and (3) ousiai, that is logically, temporally and substantially. The arguments for the priority in substance, which of course are of the most interest to us here, are four or five: (a) a mere statement that the posterior in becoming are prior in form and substance; (b) the argument based on purpose (activity is the purpose of substance); (c) the argument from eternals (these must be actualities, since potentialities are potentialities to be or not to be, 1050b6-1051a3); (d) the argument from opposites in value in chapter ix (similar to the argument from eternals, but from value opposites instead of existential opposites); (e) the argument that geometry is an activity. This last is not quite so sure (1051a20-33; see Ross' notes, vol. II, 268-73).

Whatever one thinks of these arguments—and they are certainly open to objections—they express nevertheless clearly Aristotle's position. In chapters viii and ix there is no doubt how he answers the question raised (implicitly) in Book H. Given the priority of actuality, it must be the actual mode of ousia that he considers primary, and on the basis of this preference his ontology is rightly seen as an ontology of form and the individual. On this basis also the scholastic interpretation of the Aristotlelian text is quite fair and correct. But is it the whole story?

IOTA
THE ONTOLOGY OF THE ONE

It will be recalled that, in the outline of the *Metaphysics* as a whole, Book I was segregated as a special ontology of the One, in which Aristotle discussed and dismissed an inherited tradition. That tradition had many facets, found in the philosophies of the Pythagoreans, of the Ionian physicists and Empedocles, of Parmenides and Plato. In it Oneness was still tied closely to things and to beings and Being. Units were ogkoi (bodies) of some sort (Pythagoreans), or unity was a physical substance (the physicists) or force (philotEs, Empedocles), or it was the whole immovable universe (as Parmenides was mistakenly understood). Plato's *Parmenides* challenged these primitive views, although it is doubtful that the challenge was understood, and many passages in the *Metaphysics* (e.g. the eleventh aporia, in B, iv, 1001a4-b25) indicate that it was still a mooted matter, which Aristotle was forced to deal with.

Aristotle begins his first chapter by offering his own theory of the One. This was quite original. Nothing like it is found in prior texts, if we except the implications of the Parmenides. In our terms, it is a wholly abstract treatment of the One, divorcing it utterly from the old connections to Being and beings of whatever sort. After giving examples of unity, to suneches, to holon, and hen logOi (eidei kai arithmOi), in four different kinds, he distinguishes and pursues the question: what is the essence of unity and its definition (1052b1-3)? Dio kai to heni einai to adiairetOi estin einai, hoper tode onti kai idiai chOristOi E topOi E eidei E dianoiai, E kai to holOi kai adiairetOi, malista de to metrOi einai protOi hekastou genous kai kuriOtata tou posou (1052b15-19): the essence of oneness is in indivisibility, and most of all in its being the first measure in any of the categories, especially quantity.

Having done this, Aristotle then turns and looks back. He presents some of the former theories of the One (1053b9-16), and then pauses momentarily (1053b16-1054a19) to balance the claims of the old and the new views. So chapter two:

1. former theories of the One   1053b9-16
   a. Pythagoreans
   b. physicists
2. One, like being, is a predicate, not an ousia   b16-19
3. What is the One?   b24-28
   a. some analogies   b28-a5
   b. the One is something (ti) but not an ousia   a5-9
   c. one must seek the absolute One   a9-13
   d. somehow to on and to hen mean the same   a13-19

Then he turns to the tradition again. In that tradition the One was viewed in the larger context of the contraries (tanantia). These are the subject of the rest of Book I, as is seen in the summary outline below. To appreciate the character and the force of the tradition of the contraries, one need only turn to Plato's *Parmenides*, in which they are a major feature of the discussion, or one may recall the famous Pythagorean sustoichia There is also a thinly veiled reference to the *Sophist*, 258c-259b, at one point (1054b18-22), but it is the *Parmenides*, with its exhaustive study of to hen kai talla (= to hen kai ta polla, 1054a20, 1055b27) and tanantia, that is echoed here and which represents the culmination of the old tradition in Plato's masterful challenge to it. The tanantia were closely associated with the One.

The tradition raised some problems (chapters iv and v), which Aristotle answers by returning to his original statement in the first chapter: the essence of unity is measure and indivisibility. From these follow the opposition and the contrariety of the many, measured and divisible. With this the ring is closed, so to speak, and the Book I has returned to its starting point. The remaining four chapters contain some redundancies (compare the conclusion of chapter vii, 1057b29-32, with chapter iv, 1055a27-29; and chapter viii with the latter part of chapter iii, 1054b22-35), some elucidation (chapter ix), and the characteristic anti-Platonist comment of chapter x. Here is a summary outline of Book I:

A. The One   i

   1. Aristotle's innovative analysis
     a. four kinds of unity
       1 continuous, suneches
       2 whole, holon
       3 individual, arithmOi
       4 universal, eidei
     b. the essence of unity
       1 indivisibility
       2 measure
   2. retrospect   ii
     a. former theories of the One
     b. the One is not an ousia
     c. what is the One?

B. Opposites and contraries   iii

   1. the One and the Many
   2. other contraries (3 from the traditional list)
   3. on contrariety   iv
     a. definitions
     b. relations to other kinds of opposition
       viz.: contradiction, privation
     c. all contraries are reducible to the One
       and the Many
   4. problems, hen heni enantion   v
     a. how can equal have two contraries?

b. how can the One and the Many be opposed?   vi
[Aristotle's answer:] As measure and
measured, indivisible and divisible
5. additional discussion
   a. the priority of the first contraries   vii
   b. contraries within a genus (i.e. between   viii
    species), to a genus, and outside a genus
    (parallels latter part of chapter iii)
   c. differences must be formal   ix
   d. an anti-Platonist argument: perishable   x
   and imperishable differ in kind

To recapitulate, Book I stands alone, with no constructive relation to the main tenor of the *Metaphysics*. Its role is to deal with and to dismiss a long-standing tradition of Greek speculation, one which led to no successful ontological conclusions. The debris had to be cleared from the site, as it were, to make room for a more fruitful metaphysics. Its present postion in the order of books would seem to be fortuitous. It might just as well be taken after Delta or before M, or some such arrangement. This is however a minor point, serving best only to elucidate its role.

K
A TRANSITION

Book K is clearly divided into two main parts: (1) chapters i through viii, 1065a26, are a recapitulation of parts of Book A (in only two and a half lines), B, Gamma and E, but (2) chapters viii, 1065a26 through xii are a series of extracts from the *Physics*, Books II, III and V. What is the explanation of this seeming strange combination? And of its presence here?

The question, when was this book composed? addressed by Jaeger, does not concern us at this moment. If it is a primitive version of A, B, Gamma, and E, in its first part, for example, still it was put here at some later date; someone thought it belonged here. This is as significant as if it were specially prepared at that later date. And why was it combined with the extracts from the *Physics*? Was it to serve as a point of transition in the overall scheme: a recapitulation of the earlier gains and a new departure in a new direction? The first part does point backward to the earlier books, while the second part points forward to Book Lambda and to the ontology of the moving and final causes. Is it straining the evidence to suggest that Book K may have been meant to be some sort of transition?

With this in mind our gaze is now directed to chapter vii (recapitulation of E, i). This chapter is about the relationship between the sciences. Attention may be arrested by the neat organization of the theoretical, productive and practical sciences, and by Aristotle's effort to classify the theoretical sciences by means of the criteria of motion and separation (kinEton, akinEton, chOriston, achOriston). All this seems so neat and handy at first sight, but closer inspection, especially of E, i, the parallel of K, vii, reveals that it is also a bit fuzzy. In E, i, Aristotle changes his mind about the classifications in the course of the chapter. The objects of physics *are not* separate at 1025b28, and then they *are* separate at

1026a13-14. The objects of mathematics present a case explicitly admitted to be not so clear. Some are separate (1026a9-10); some, not (a15). All this has been commented on amply by Schwegler, Ross, Jaeger and Merlan, so that there is little need to add to it except to suggest that our attention may have been diverted to a sideshow.

Is not the main point of this chapter and its parallel, E, i, to ask about the nature of the *first* science? What is this science about? How does its object differ from the objects of others? It is ***not*:** how do we organize all the sciences neatly—as tempting an undertaking as that might be. This is Aristotle speaking, not Hugh of St. Victor or Thomas Aquinas or some other scholastic of the cathedral age. He is separating here, not synthesizing. If this difference seems subtle, it is nevertheless important: it directs our attention to ambiguities and difficulties in determining what direction the first science is to take. To ask what this science is about—if this is the purpose of K—is to discover that it is about two utterly different classes of objects, both of which are chOriston and akinEton. There are (1) the chOriston and akinEton of intellectual abstraction, of logos, of definition, of form and matter disjoined from each other. And there are (2) the chOriston and akinEton of the Unmoved Prime Mover, beyond all motion, but reached by consideration of and defined in terms of the physical world. These two words (chOriston and akinEton), both ambiguous, are the criteria of distinction used in K to define the objects of the first science. An unchanging, eternal Idea or an abstraction is motionless. So also is the Unmoved Prime Mover, in a different sense. One is in the context of the intellectual, non-physical world; the other, in the context of the physical. Each is also separate in a different sense, the same different senses as above. The Idea, or form and matter, pure intellectibles, on the one hand, and the Unmoved Prime Mover, on the other, are two utterly different kinds of permanence and separation. The dichotomy of the physical-metaphysical has simply been pushed back one more stage, so that metaphysics contains ***within*** itself the same distinction that was used to separate it from physics. If K, vii, indicates this, then its place between the two ontologies that embody this difference would seem quite appropriate. So would its position nearly at the center of K, if K as a whole reflects this division. This it certainly does, the first half being a recapitulation of the intellectual and formal ontology, the second half being an introduction to physics.

The introduction to physics in the second half of K is a collection of extracts from the early books of the *Physics*. Is there anything peculiar about those? Beginning with a section on chance and the accidental, they might seem to fit somehow with the earlier part of chapter viii. This could be either unintentional (unconscious suggestion) or intentional (to effect a smooth transition), and it has therefore little significance to me. But viewed at large the extracts from the *Physics* in K, viii (1065a26)—xii, after this brief account of accidental being and chance (a26-b4), are devoted to two topics: change (motion) and the infinite. An outline displays this:

A. Accidental being and chance   1065a26-b4

B. Change and Motion   chap. ix

   1. potentiality and actuality (brief allusion)   b5-7
   2. change and motion always occur in one of the categories
   3. are the actualization of the potential   b14-1066a7
   4. other theories criticized   a7-17
   5. why it is difficult to understand what motion is, and why it seems indefinite   a17-26
   6. one same actualization in mover and moved   a26-34

C. The infinite   chap. x

   1. definitions: what cannot be or is not traversed, etc.   a35-b1

2. is not a separate, absolute being	b1-7
3. is a property, not an element	b7-11
4. is not actual	b11-21
5. is not in sensibles	b21-1067a33
6. infinities of magnitude, motion and times differ	a33-37

D. Change and motion (resumed) — chap. xi

1. three kinds: accidental, partial, absolute	b1-7
2. elements of change: mover, moved, time, ex hou and eis ho	b7-9
3. elements *not* of change: forms, properties, place	b9-12
4. three kinds of change in respect to the substrate (change distinguished from coming-into-being and destruction)	b12-1068a1
5. recap	a1-7
6. change only occurs in the three primary categories: quality, quantity, place	chap. xii a7-b20

E. The unchanged — b20-25

F. Sundry definition — b26-1069a14

All this is relatively introductory and general stuff, of the sort needed for any study of change and motion, as distinguished from the special problems of *Physics*, VI, inspired by Zeno, and from the metaphysical treatment of *Physics* VIII which parallels Lambda, *Metaphysics*. (Book VII is suspect.) It seems possible that these latter chapters of K, *Metaphysics*, are intended to perform a function similar to one of their functions in the *Physics*. That is, they introduce a "metaphysics" of motion. This is of course from our point of view a paradox, motion being ordinarily a province of physics. But this is a hypothesis. It would help explain to some extent the transitional role of Kappa. For the nonce the main support for such a hypothesis is found not in the detailed lines of the book itself, as much as in the way that it fits as a whole, however crudely, into the structure of the treatise as a whole. It has all the appearance of a transition between the two major ontologies of the *Metaphysics*, when looked at in this manner.

LAMBDA
THE "PHYSICAL METAPHYSICS" & THE UNMOVED PRIME MOVER

What is the structure of this book? How is the thought to be organized? The key to the structure is given in a passage at the end of the first chapter, 1069a30-b2, a passage which has somehow been rendered obscure. Whether this obscurity is accountable to the manuscript tradition or to plain poor composition is undecidable. The emendations of the first two or three lines, 1069a30-32, give little difficulty. It is the subdivision of the ousia akinEtos (motionless substance, line a33) that is liable to confuse the reader, because it is really a parenthetical aside, of subordinate value, not to be taken as part of the main thought. The lines, 1069a34-38, are best ignored at first. The three kinds of ousia which this passage deliberately highlights are:

1. sensible
   a. eternal
   b. perishable
2. motionless

This division is explicitly confirmed, fortunately, by the opening lines of chapter vi: epei d' Esan treis ousia, duo men hai phusikai mia d' hE akinEtos...(1071b3-4). From this we may infer that although there are three kinds of ousiai there are two *main divisions* or kinds: (1) sensible, and (2) motionless ("or some say separate"—line 34). These two main kinds provide the key to the structure of Book Lambda. Although we will have reason later to question this, it will stand.

The book commences with an introductory chapter which first establishes the priority of ousia in our investigation, and then establishes the main kinds, in the passage just referred to. The balance of the book, chapters ii—x, treat of ousia under these two main headings, excepting chapters iv and v. These form a bridge between the two divisions. Thus the structure of the book is given summarily as follows:

I. Introductory: ousia (chapter i)

    A. Its priority
    B. Its kinds
        1. sensible
        2. motionless, separate

II. Sensible substance (chapters ii, iii)

III. An aporia (problem): are the causes and
    elements the same for all ousiai, or not?
    This is the "bridge" (chapters iv, v).

IV. Motionless, separate substance (chapters vi—x)

Our attention is here directed to the apparent anomaly, the departure from the obvious smooth flow of thought in section III above: the "aporia." When we come to it in the text we also find that it is organized within itself after a fashion quite different from its surrounding context. What is the role of this transition between the two main topics?

Aristotle's discussion of this "aporia" is far from simple. To begin with, it has itself two main divisions: A. the discussion of the two causes and principles of sensible substance already identified in section II (chap. ii, 1069b3-15, 32-34) and well known to us from prior use in Books Z and Eta, form and matter; and B. the discussion of two other causes and principles also mentioned in section II (chap. ii, 1069b15-32) and known to us from Book Theta, potentiality and actuality. These do not stand out quite so clearly as causes and elements in chapter ii, owing to their manner of presentation there; the passage sounds like an amplification of the discussion of matter and form

However that may be, the discussion in chapters iv and v of the "aporia" clearly shows this main division (A., B. as indicated), and potentiality and actuality are clearly brought to the fore as elements and causes of ousiai. This will prove significant shortly, because of an important difference in the answer given to the problem in either case (A. or B.).

In the case of A., form and matter, the answer ultimately chosen (1070b10-21) is: yes and no. In one sense, a general and universal sense (tOi analogon)—cf. also 1070a32 for the equivalence of this phrase with katholou), they are the same for all. In another sense, i.e. in each particular instance, they are not the same.

In the case of B., potentiality and actuality, the same observation may be made. They too may be treated either as universals (abstractions) or as particulars in any given instance, from individual to individual (chap. v, 1071a4-5), *but* (adds Aristotle) they also have another, different way of being different! alla kai tauta alla te allois kai allOs (1071a5-6) is an arresting bit of rhetoric. They differ not only in the manner that matter and form differ, i.e. particularly in each instance, but they also differ hOsper anthrOpou aition ta te stoicheia…ti allo exO hoion ho patEr (1071a13-15), i.e. as an external mover that has the power to bring something into actual being, *silicet* a father, a son. This is a meaning of dunamis, etc. Lambda , xii, 1019a15-20, 1020a1-6; Theta, i, 1046a1-11) different from Aristotle's special sense in Theta, vi for which latter we usually use in English the terms, potentiality and actuality, instead of the terms, power and act (or activity or action). It is the power to move something, alla kinounta, as Aristotle immediately makes clear (1017a17).

By means of this ambiguity of meaning, Aristotle has diverted our attention from the question of universals and particulars (really what we call the question of abstraction) to the question of motion (movement, change). As he says directly: some things are expressed as universals, some are not 1071a17-18). We have moved from the one situation to the other. In place of the question of being and substance as universals or particulars, we now have the question of being and substance as changeable, moveable, etc., or not. The discussion of potentiality and power has been the occasion for a switch. Looking back now, we can also see that the same transformation of the terms of discussion was effected in the discussion of form and matter just before (i.e. in A.). There the question of motion was introduced quite abruptly at the end of chapter iv (1070b22-35), without any such excuse of an ambiguity of terms as occurs in chapter v. We are simply told that there are not only indwelling causes, but external moving ones. Thus it appears that this addition of a new dimension to the discussion of causes and elements of ousia is quite intentional.

In sum, the function of chapters iv and v is quite important: it is to effect again the transformation of the investigation from one about indwelling causes to one about moving causes (to use Aristotle's very own terms, 1070b22-23). But this is not all. The investigation of indwelling causes turns here explicitly upon the question of universals. The investigation of moving causes does not, or rather, if it does, it does in a very different sense. It turns upon externals, and leads ultimately to an abstraction or universal of a wholly different kind: the Unmoved Prime Mover, to prOton kinoun akinEton.

Universal, abstract, separate, to katholou, chOriston, mean many things (pollachOs legontai). How aware was Aristotle of this? The transition, as we said above, seems intentional, but was he aware of all its implications?

What are these implications?

At the very least they are that we are now faced (as the remainder of Lambda, chapters vi—x, makes clear) with a quite different kind of metaphysics than we have been faced with before (excepting perhaps intimations of it in K, and a single exceptional remark at the very end of Book Gamma). There are two kinds of metaphysics: (1) the metaphysics of indwelling causes (ta enuparchonta aitia, 1070b22) and universals, which command the major share of the attention of chapters ii—iv, and hark back to earlier books of the *Metaphysics* (Z—Theta), and (2) the metaphysics of external, moving causes (alla kai tOn ektos hoion to kinoun, 1070b22-23), which command the attention of chapter v and of the remainder of Lambda, chapters vi—x.

Certainly others have sometimes not been aware of this transition and metamorphosis of metaphysics, because many commentators have gone to great lengths to integrate, unify, connect these two parts, making Lambda the conclusion of a process begun as far back as E, and identifying the ousia of Z—Eta with the prime mover of Lambda. This way the very sharp break is ignored.

What shall we call these two distinct kinds of metaphysics, if other than what Aristotle has already called them? Some have called the second kind (tOn ektos hoion to kinoun) a theology, on account of the divine character explicitly attributed to the Unmoved Prime Mover by Aristotle in the latter half of chapter vii. Some may note that it is a metaphysics much closer to physics in a sense, a sort of physical metaphysics (a hybrid of some kind), on account of its preoccupation with motion. We may also easily note the parallel between the two metaphysics and the two sets of Aristotle's four causes, (1) form and matter, and (2) efficient and final. Thus we may call them each by the respective names: a metaphysics of form and matter, and a metaphysics of efficient and final causes. In any case, Lambda is hardly a theology in our usual sense of the term or in Aristotle's, nor is metaphysics just another branch of physics, close as it is to both of those. Nor does calling it the science of the four causes seem to fill the bill. There is something special about metaphysics that separates its treatment of all of these topics from all other treatments of them. It is this: metaphysics deals with universals and abstractions primarily, doing so in the two ways that conform to the two meanings of those terms. (1) We may abstract mentally, as we do when we speak of form and matter, or (2) we may abstract physically, as we do when we speak of a first mover beyond the heavens. In both cases we abstract, but in one mentally, in the other physically. If abstraction can create two kinds of world for us, now we find that it can do it two ways. In short the dichotomy which abstraction is capable of producing applies to the producer, abstraction, itself. We have simply moved back another stage. ara badizei eis apeiron;

M
APPENDIX ON NUMBERS AND IDEAS

That this book is divided into two distinct parts at 1086b21, the first part late, the second part early in date of composition, has been demonstrated by Werner Jaeger. One may ask both (1) what this division signifies, and (2) why they were put together at all. In any case we will proceed to consider the first part first, following the text just as received.

THE FIRST PART (Chapter i—ix, 1086a21)

M opens with a remark that seems to throw our whole exposition of Lambda into question: peri men oun to tEs tOn aisthEtOn ousias eirEtai tis estin…" now we have said what the substance of sensibles is," etc. (1076a8-12). One might take this to mean that Lambda is concerned with sensibles, and only now in M are we to take up the question of separate and motionless and eternal substance. After all, it might be argued that Lambda is mostly about movables and motion, even in its latter chapters (vi—x), excepting only the Unmoved Prime Mover, and that even this is derived from consideration of motion; *ergo* it is a study of motion and sensibles and such. But this argument will not stand. Aristotle explicitly states (1071b1-5) that Lambda, vi—x, is about motionless, eternal substance. This is also clearly the objective of the discussion, which may serve to label it just as well as may the route by which it was achieved.

One may point out that M, i—ix (1086a21) is a piece from a different period, an interruption in the continuous composition of K, Lambda, M, x—x, and N. This may explain it procedurally, but what substantively might have allowed this to happen? Why could this insertion be made with impunity? What allows the confusion about the "natures" of sensibles and separate substances, that in turn allows an uncertainty on our part about Lambda, vi—x, whether it is about separates and immovables, or not; or whether M, i—ix, is about these? What, in brief, is deficient in our understanding of separates and immovables, that allows us to accept this insertion here of a revision in an old continuum?

All these questions are quickly answered by repeating the observation that there is an ambiguity in the terms, "separate, motionless," chOristos, akinEtos. They may all be used in two ways:

A. "Separate" may mean

1. physically separate, i.e. separated physically to another place, or
2. mentally separate, i.e. separated from all physical things, being mental,

B. "Motionless" may mean

1. physically motionless, but physical otherwise, or
2. mentally motionless, because not physical.

"Separate" and "motionless," in other words are sometimes used of entities in a physical scheme, sometimes used of entities not in any physical scheme but in fact quite opposed to such. The criteria are in the first case physical; in the second, mental. Words that are themselves sometimes used to distinguish the mental and the physical are themselves also subject to the same division that they are being used to identify. There are yet more possibilities for confusion: Aristotle's Unmoved Prime Mover, ho protos ouranos, e.g. the prime example of 1. physical motionlessness and separation, takes on characteristics of 2. pure mentality as soon as one considers it at any length. The route to it in Lambda nevertheless is 1. physical. Once again it seems as if body and mind are primary data that can neither be separated nor reduced to one another, a paradox if ever there was one.

Lambda, vi—x, deals with one kind of motionless, separate substance; M i—x, with the other. As long as the ambiguity of the notions allows a place for both kinds, the two treatments of the subject can be placed side by side, not perhaps without causing perplexity, but with impunity, with consistency to the paradoxical data.

M, i—x, then, deals with motionless and separate substance of the other kind: the mental. Other than the subject of Lambda. It is in this wise that they take their place after Lambda. M deals with the two subspecies of this kind that had been recognized (whether accepted or rejected) by Aristotle's predecessors and contemporaries: Ideas and mathematicals (number, etc.) (1076a16 ff.). So it begins immediately, citing three contemporary schools of thought about these (1076a19-22). Then it gives forthwith (1076a22-32) the program of inquiry and the summary outline of the next five chapters:

I. Mathematicals by themselves (ii, iii)
II. Ideas by themselves (iv, v)
III. Numbers *and* Ideas (vi).

The discussion of numbers and Ideas continues beyond this, but at this point the conclusion is reached that all the existing theories of the various schools are impossible. The point is especially made by Aristotle that they are *not* separate. It is made in many ways with respect to both mathematicals and Ideas. In treating of mathematicals in chapter iii, Aristotle makes his own statement that these have a peculiar kind of existence of their own (tropon tina...hEi toiadi, 1077b16-22). The objects, he says, of mathematics are neither sensible nor separate, *but treated as if they are separate* (1078a3-4, 17-22, italics added). The objections to the separation of Ideas in chapters iv and v are numerous.

Chapter vi takes numbers and Ideas together and goes through all the contemporary theories again, rejecting them all. But it raises also a new consideration: are numbers and Ideas asumblEtoi or sumblEtoi? These are difficult words to translate. The dictionary (Liddell, Scott, Jones, ed. 1968) gives us for these terms: "not addible, not comparable, not commensurable, not capable of combination" (viz.: any of the arithmetical methods of combination), and the opposites. Let me suggest that for the twentieth century man the industrial notion of interchangeable parts may also supply a fruitful analogy. In any case a fundamental antagonism between Ideas and numbers, as current theories then viewed them, is raised by Aristotle here: Ideas were seen as unique; numbers were not, at least not always. The commonness of numbers is obvious to the common man, and there was at that time some question and argument about numbers, as to whether they were "incomparable," like Ideas, or "comparable" as in common use. In other words, were numbers ideal or mathematical? This argument revealed a weakness in the theories of Ideas and numbers: in some respects the two are alike, yet there was this incompatibility. The obvious everyday comparability and countability of numbers conflicted with their uniqueness, if they were like Ideas; or otherwise the Idea theory must be wrong. Aristotle's sixth chapter of M is aimed at these inconsistencies.

It is followed in chapters vii—ix by a closer examination of the question of numbers and what they are. It seems quite natural that this should lead next to the investigation of monads—of what we in modern parlance are apt to call units—which are the building blocks, as we would say, or the beginning, the principle, the least of all numbers, as Aristotle says (Bonitz, *Index*, p. 471). Are *they* "comparable" or "incomparable?" This is chapter vii. At the same time Aristotle's method has shifted from a topical organization to a personally directed one. Late in the sixth chapter he is more explicitly attacking contemporary schools of thought. The monads of chapter vii are Platonic. In chapter viii the theories of Speusippus, Xenocrates and the Pythagoreans are dealt with. Only the Pythagoreans are named explicitly, but the other identifications are plain enough to be widely accepted. After additional general and specific arguments in the rest of chapters viii and ix, Aristotle comes again to his final conclusion: that separate number and magnitude are impossible (1085b34-37), and so are all the theories that espouse them (1085b37-1086a18).

Much of M is polemical and negative, to be sure, but in all this Aristotle's positive doctrine should not be missed. There are no separate Ideas or numbers, but numbers have a peculiar kind of existence. Although not separate, they are treated as if they were (chapter iii). The same thought is repeated elsewhere, in *On the Soul*, Gamma, vii, 431b13-19. As for Ideas, he does not go so far as to say such a thing, although one might not be blamed for drawing the same conclusion. One might also be justified in asking why Aristotle is not so explicit about the Ideas? Is he less sure of himself? It is a mistake to think that what is obvious to us might be as obvious to him, or that he wishes to make it so obvious. Many personal and circumstantial considerations may have intruded here. What is certain is that Aristotle's remark is made only about numbers. We have tried to summarize the text as it is.

Numbers (and only possibly, Ideas) are not separate, but are treated as if they were. What does this mean? Notice that *at no time has Aristotle made it explicitly clear, in such terms as we have above, just what he means by "separate,"* just what kind of separation (physical or mental) he means. Yet it is implicitly clear that he has all along been objecting to physical separation (viz.: the absolute man and horse of 997b5-12, 1040b30-34, 1060a15-18, etc.). His "treated as though they were separate" is nothing less than the other kind of separation, mental separation. That is what it means, although this is the best he can do to express this yet. Again, it is the mind-body distinction that Aristotle is appealing to, we are now in a position to see. This is the principle and axiom of his metaphysics that he repeatedly comes back to without naming it explicitly in such words as we use today.

M contains more about number and the mathematicals than any other book so far. This fact may be called upon to account for the place of M in the scheme of the *Metaphysics* as a whole. The problem of being and substance is a problem of abstraction. In the core of the *Metaphysics*, Z, Eta and Theta, Aristotle's solution of this is tendered with his revision of the Form theory, namely his studies of form and matter, and of potentiality and actuality. In K and Lambda, a solution, probably an older one, is tendered in terms of motion and the moving causes, efficient and final. That it is a remnant of early Aristotelian thought should not disqualify it from the interest and attention of the earnest metaphysician. But it is different, distinct in its own archai as in its product, a different sort of separate and motionless being. Now in M the problem is approached from a third angle, that of mathematics and number. The interest in and developlment of mathematics, in and around the Academy in the mid-fourth century, makes the suggestion of this approach hardly surprising. That there is some kind of kinship between Ideas and numbers is also obvious. That the precise relationship and natures of them were difficult to determine for those early thinkers should again not surprise us, nor that there were many false starts. Aristotle's insight in M, iii, that numbers have a peculiar kind of existence, and that they are neither sensible nor separate in one sense, but are separate in another ("as if one placed them separate," 1078a17-22), was a very happy one. It leads us on the right track. It remains only to reflect further upon just what this act of "setting aside" is, and what status we are to accord to it. Further, the insight may easily (for us) be transferred to Ideas. Aristotle's study of number here contributes directly and in a third distinct fashion in the *Metaphysics* to a theory of Ideas, a theory of the ultimate of all Ideas, i.e. of Being, and a theory of what will in later times be called abstraction. That he did not lay all this out explicitly need not surprise us, either.

THE SECOND PART (Chapter ix, 1086a21—x, end)

The remainder of chapter ix causes no great difficulty. In a neat and explicit transition the investigation is turned to the principles, causes and elements of non-sensible substances other than numbers and mathematicals in general, in short to Platonic Ideas. But the problem is after all the same: the reconciliation of separability, universality and individuality (uniqueness) of Ideas is analogous to the reconciliation of separability and inseparability, and of comparability and incomparability, which dominate the earlier chapters of M. This problem of separability, universality and individuality of Ideas as raised by the Platonic theory is in this part introduced generally first at 1086a32-34. Then it is stated in greater detail in chapter x.

Chapter x itself is difficult at first sight. Careful inspection however reveals a very precise structure that gives evidence of Aristotle's dialectical mind at work. First there is the detailed statement of the problem. Then there is the solution of it.

The Statement of the problem

This takes the shape of a "Chinese box" of dilemmas, that is a dilemma within a dilemma within a dilemma within a dilemma! These may be identified as follows (briefly):

1. There are Ideas, 1086b14, tois legousi,
    a. not separate substances, b16, ei men gar,
    b. are separate substances, b19, an de tis,
        1 their elements are individual, b20, ei men gar,
        2 their elements are universal, b37, alla mEn,
            a substances are universal, b37, E,
            b non-substance prior to substance, a1, E,
2. There are not Ideas, 1086b15, tois mE legousin, and 1087a7-8, ei de mEthen...kai mEthen...

The reader may note that Ross and Jaeger disagree on the text of 1087a1, our innermost dilemma. In this instance Ross' rendering seems most satisfactory, especially in view of the context. All the horns of these dilemmas eventuate in unsatisfactory results.

1. either
    a. they do away with substance as we [Platonists] understand it, OR
    b. either

     1 there can be nothing but elements, OR

     2 either

          a there are no individual substances, OR

          b non-substance is prior to substance,

    2. OR there will be an unlimited number of like [unlike?] syllables (i.e. by analogy: substances).

The solution

This is given in dialectical distinctions commencing at 1087a10. First of all universals are distinguished from Platonic Ideas. The universals are *not* separate substances, as the Ideas are supposed to be, and it is these (universals) that are the object of knowledge, to de tEn epistEmEn einai katholou pasan, hOste anagkaion einai kai tas tOn ontOn archas katholou einai kai mE ousias kekOrismenas. Again Aristotle does not distinguish explicitly what kind of separation he intends here, but in the context his meaning is clear: it is the physical sort of separation that Ideas were said to have. It is the universals that have the separability of the other, mental kind, connected as they are with knowledge. None of this is fully clear yet in his language, or even as clear as it was in his "not-separate-but-treated-as-separate" numbers of chapter iii.

There remains, to be solved secondly, after the dichotomy of separability and inseparability, the problem of universality and individuality, echei men malist' aporian tOn lechthentOn, 1087a13. How do we know both, unless there are two kinds of knowledge? Another important distinction, for which Aristotle makes use of his potentiality-actuality theory.

How to evaluate all this? If it is right that this is an earlier version of the *Metaphysics*, it does seem as though these distinctions point toward the later distinctions of the earlier chapters of M, and all point toward the primary mind-body distinction of a yet later era. The last seems implicit, although not yet explicit in Aristotle.

M is a sort of appendix, largely an *ad hominem* argument, directed at Aristotle's immediate rivals in the contemporary schools. It is a prototype of the responses (*Respondeo Dicendum...*, etc.) of Thomas Aquinas' *Summa Theologiae*.

N
APPENDIX ON NUMBERS AND OPPOSITES

What is the difference between M and N, aside from the fact that they may have been composed at different times in Aristotle's career (Jaeger)? Both books feature number, but in different ways. M treats of number and Ideas, and their relation. We just saw now how M uses the study of number to throw light upon the nature of abstraction and possibly of Ideas. N, on the other hand, treats of number and opposite first principles, not (as it states at the very outset) the old opposites of the physicists, hot and cold, wet and dry, Love and Strife, and so forth, but the newer opposites of the Academy and contemporary Pythagoreans. There were several sets of these offered by various individuals: to mega kai to mikron, and to hen kai to aoristos duas, by Plato in his lectures, to hen kai talla in the *Parmenides*, sameness and difference in the *Sophist*. Other variations were: to hen kai to plEthos (Speusippus?), the equal and the unequal, and so forth. These pairs of concepts were being used to explain the generation and nature of number, multiplicity and the physical world. Book N is Aristotle's record and criticism of that fruitless endeavor. It includes the late Pythagorean theories which relate number to the physical world, also. This seems quite appropriate. This is what N is all about, in contrast to M's concern with the relation of number and Ideas. N is about number and the physical world. N, too, is a sort of appendix, a response to lingering contemporary doctrines.

CONCLUSION

We have conducted here a rather intense study of a novel sort. Intense, because it has required of the writer and the reader a close following of the actual Greek text of the *Metaphysics*. That is no easy task. Novel, in the assumption and method that it has used. The assumption was that the *Metaphysics* as received by us is an organized text as a whole and in nearly all of its parts, and is itself part of a larger context of philosophical development. The organization was elucidated by following the text book by book, chapter by chapter, sometimes even line by line, and outlining it.

Little has been said yet about the larger context of which the *Metaphysics* is a part, other than occasional hints. These may now be drawn together and inspected. They will provide the second key to the understanding of the *Metaphysics*.

That Aristotle's inquiry is well-grounded in the prior developments of Greek speculation is utterly obvious at the outset in Book A, and at numerous points in the ensuing books (e.g. a, i; Lambda, v, etc.). That it takes notice of contemporary discussions has just been seen in Books M and N. What is not so obvious is its special relationship to a particular strand of prior and current speculation, a strand best represented (though probably by no means limited) by the speculations of Parmenides, and of Plato in his dialogue, the *Parmenides*. This special relationship has probably been overlooked for two reasons: (1) a gross misunderstanding of Parmenides' doctrine, and (2) the extreme difficulty of the dialogue, the *Parmenides*. It accounts, among other passages, for Book I.

The *Metaphysics* is riddled with lines of a certain type which the reader usually finds most puzzling. These are lines that can quickly be found by looking in Ross' *Index verborum* or in Bonitz' *Index* for to hen kai to on, or for tanantia under enantion. There is also the curious presence of Book I as a whole. These are notions that were much discussed and disputed in pre-Aristotelian Greek speculation, but nowhere so explicitly and intensively as in the eight hypotheses of Plato's *Parmenides*. This text, which delighted the neoplatonists centuries ago, and has baffled most modern readers of it, has been interpreted in diverse ways. It has even been called a joke. But it is a very serious inquiry into the nature of abstraction. In it Plato demonstrates the difficulties involved in the conception of one particular abstraction: unity, the One, to hen. The dialogue ends with these words: "It seems that, whether there is or is not a one, both that one and the others alike are and are not, and appear and do not appear to be, all manner of things in all manner of ways, with respect to themselves and to one another." He could have played much the same game with to on, Being, and possibly with any abstraction. It is characteristic of Plato that often he was at his most playful when he was being most serious. This was a most serious challenge. It was directed against the words of Parmenides himself, as understood at that time, eon...nun estin homou pan, hen...(DK VIII, 3ff.), against the core of his supposed doctrine, that the universe is one.

Plato understood, it seems, something about Parmenides that most of his contemporaries and everyone since have failed to understand: that the being of Parmenides was not the whole of the universe, as all the others thought he meant. Simply stated, Parmenides was just not that dumb. What he must have been thinking was the oldest effort on record to conceive of an abstraction, in this case the particular abstraction: pure Being. This is what Plato saw. There is no way to **prove** that this was the case, of course, but it is the only one that makes sense, and it is circumstantial evidence of it, that Plato's dialogue, the *Parmenides*, deals with abstractions. Where Parmenides had, however tentatively, conceived of one abstraction, estin, Plato conceived of a number of them. He also saw the difficulties in understanding just what they were and just how to deal with them. Parmenides' estin and eon became Plato's ontOs on and auto to ____, the Ideas. Some of the difficulties are explicitly raised in the *Parmenides*. This connection of the dialogue and the man after whom it is named was soon forgotten in the general misunderstanding of Parmenides' meaning.

Plato's Ideas, too, were apparently misunderstood. These notions were so novel that that should be no surpise to us. Nowhere does Aristotle reveal so typically his understanding of Plato's Ideas as in the passage in the *Metaphysics*, B, ii, 997b5-12: auto gar anthrOpon phasin einai kai hippon kai hugieian, allo d' ouden, paraplEsion poiountes tois theous men einai phaskousin anthrOpoeideis de, oute gar hekeinoi ouden allo epoioun E anthrOpous aidious, outh' houtoi ta eidei all' E aisthEta aidia. "They say nothing other than that there are absolute men, absolute horses, absolute health, doing like those who say that there are gods but in human form. They are making nothing else than eternal men. Their Ideas are nothing but eternal sensibles." This is hardly an isolated metaphor, this reference to men and horses. They appear twice again in the *Metaphysics* at 1040b30-34 and 1060a15-18. In a word, Plato's Ideas were hypostasized. They had become things, just as Parmenides' one Being had become one world. It was shown again how difficult it is to hold on to an abstraction, and to refuse to clothe it with a material nature. Aristotle had every right to deplore the Ideas that had succumbed to such a process. His criticism of Plato would be just, if this were what Plato stood for. The result of course is the *Metaphysics*. This work is first and foremost an effort to repudiate an ontology of hypostasized Ideas, and to rediscover abstractions, to replace Forms with form. Thus the *Metaphysics* grew out of a context of problems and discussions that are represented especially well by Parmenides and the *Parmenides*. Parmenides' estin, after becoming Plato's ontOs on, became Aristotle's ousia.

These were not the only important elements of the context. There remained primitive notions that competed with these new ones in the controversies that flourished around these questions of unity and abstraction. Some of these are attributed to the Pythagoreans, but may well have been more widespread. Units were substantial monads; in the extreme case, ogkoi, bulks, particles. Numbers were associated with things. Traces of such primitive views are found in the *Metaphysics* and *Physics*. These were the negative, or shadow side of the context, the tug of primitive tradition that had also overcome the doctrines of Parmenides and Plato, it seems, and against which Aristotle had to state again the claims for abstraction, as he does in Book I for the particular case of unity, and in the treatise as a whole for form. Aristotle's form is Plato's Forms retrieved from the realm of men and horses like gods in human form, eternal sensibles. It is abstracted once again. In such a complete context of light and shadow we see the great aim of the *Metaphysics*.

The third key to the understanding of the *Metaphysics* is the placing of it in the context of subsequent western philosophical traditions. Plotinus' great synthesis of Platonic and Aristotelian metaphysics, and the success of the neoplatonic tradition for so many centuries (ten or twelve at least) is an indication of the failure of both Plato's and Aristotle's efforts. For Plato and Aristotle had tried each in turn to come to grips with the process of abstraction, to say what abstractions were, and how they worked. But such efforts were exceedingly precarious, and it seems that they had to be made all over again. Both the *Parmenides* and the *Metaphysics* lent themselves to peculiar and strange interpretations in the re-doing. The One of the *Parmenides* was hypotasized by the neoplatonists in their own distinctive way. The form from the *Metaphysics* was elevated to a special status with a special claim upon being, as over against matter and the "composite" (to sunolon). The text of the *Metaphysics* had made this possible, to be sure, since Aristotle did appear to ascribe ontological precedence to form at many points. But careful meditation upon that text will reveal a distinction to be made. In his inquiry into the principles of being, whether at the level of on or at the level of ousia, Aristotle repeatedly states his quest for on hupokeimenon, being as substrate, as well as to ti En einai, being as essence. Being *is* matter as well as form, and there *is* such an intelligible that is abstract, matter: hulE noetE. The answers that Aristotle comes up in his quest clearly seem to favor essence and form. To this extent he seems to repudiate the substrate and the matter. This is the Platonist Aristotle emerging. It is a choice that was his to make, but it represents a retrogression, a plain failure to persevere in his original program. It is like Gilbert Murray's "failure of nerve" (*Five Stages of Greek Religion*, chapter iv) after a fashion. We are still entitled to ask the original question which he asked: what is being *qua* being, ousia, as a substrate of all particular beings?

Well might he have failed! It is the point at which every other philosopher has failed: the paradoxical simultaneous connection *and* separation of mind and world. Rene Descartes' famous *cogito ergo sum* proved the existence of a thinking being, but it failed to prove the further claims that Descartes made for it: the world, not to mention God. John Locke, the British empiricist, was forced to admit that "whether there be anything more than barely that idea in our minds, whether we can thence certainly infer the existence of anything without us which corresponds to that idea, is that whereof some men think that there may be a question made (*Essay Concerning Human Understanding*, IV, ii, 14). The knowledge of the existence of any other thing, we can have only by sensation…For, the having the idea of anything in our mind no more proves the existence of that thing than the picture of a man evidences his being in the world…(IV, xi,1)." George Berkeley was and is reputed to have made the whole world nothing but the product of our minds, but he vehemently denies this in *Three Dialogues between Hylas and Philonous* (*Works*, ed. Luce and Jessop, ι. 237). David Hume was and is reputed to have proven that there is no proof from cause to effect, but when he restated this proof in his *Abstract of A Treatise of Human Nature*, he revealed that this proof is no proof at all. have discussed these failures to connect mind and body (for that is what they are) by proving the existence of the world, or perceiving the activities of the mind, in some detail in a monograph (unpublished) entitled *Berkeley's Tree*, written in 1977, and will not repeat them here. The point is that all these men, Aristotle and all the rest, were up against an insoluble problem.

What was this problem as Aristotle faced it? Let us try to restate it as simply as possible, once more.

Parmenides' One Being may have been a first dim recognition of an abstraction, but if it was, the hold on it was too tenuous to be retained. With Plato's Form theory, or Ideas, a stronger hold upon abstractions was gained, but this too seems to have been inadequate. Their relation to concrete things was not explained satisfactorily, and they were easily hypostasized into "eternal sensibles" (aisthEta aidia). Aristotle tried a third time. He sought the Forms not outside material things in the manner that Plato was held to have done, that is in the usual physical or local sense of "outside." He sought them as form within things, combined with matter in ta sunola. For a physical separation of Forms he substituted a mental separation of form and matter. The two were separable only by an intellectual analysis. You never actually found them separate. But this only avoided one kind of separation to fall into another. His form and his matter were still utterly irreconcilable with each other, when ta sunola were analyzed, when form and matter were studied themselves. It is no surprise if he was forced into choosing between them when looking for a single priority. What is more, each of them also would split into separate and irreconcilable kinds, as in the case of hulE aisthEtE and hulE noEtE. (There is also form and form, intellectual and material.) Neither the intelligible (mental) nor the sensible (physical) could be explained in terms of the other, nor could the use of both terms be avoided. They were separate and united.

There was no getting away from this. Dos moi pou stO kai kinO tEn gEn! There was no escape. It is hardly surprising that the *Metaphysics* resolved itself into two metaphysics, and we got the ontology of form and the ontology of the Unmoved Prime Mover.

Aristotle appears to avoid this by assigning priority to form. But this was an arbitrary choice on his part, one by the way that merely reflects his Platonic origins. It is not the product of careful analysis that characterizes much of the rest of the *Metaphysics*. It does not adhere to his original intent, and the ultimate intent of all true ontology: to explain what on hE on, being *qua* being, is. Perhaps his localizing the search in one kind of being *qua* being, that is in ousia, was already a step away from his original intent, because this ousia, what we now call substance, tended even more easily to become substances. It seems closer to ta kath' hekasta, whether or not we are always aware of it. We were warned against such tendencies in Book Gamma.

The difficulty that Aristotle faced is the same difficulty that everyone has faced, before and since his time. Form and matter, Idea and thing, mind and body are radically different and separate entities that are also inseparable. They have nothing in common excepting they always occur together. They are separable only mentally, not physically. And the opposite is true. All this is of course a tautology and an impossible contradiction.

So Aristotle failed, as Plato had failed, and as others have failed who have since addressed themselves to the resolution of the mind-body problem, seeking one consistent explanation. The nominalists and realists of the twelfth century, and then Descartes, Locke, Berkely, Hume, William James, Gilbert Ryle, all of them have failed. Why? Why did Aristotle fail?

The problem is insoluble.

Why is it insoluble?

If we ask for proof, proof is only an intellectual act, a product of the mind. If we ask for evidence of the senses, who feels or hears or sees or smells or tastes himself, or anyone else, think? The complete metaphysics that would unite these two realms is impossible. But somehow they are connected, since, so far as we know, when the body perishes, the brain perishes with it, the brain with which we identify the mental. Yet we cannot explain this connection; we only know that it is.

It does no good to deny (with the ascetic or the neoplatonist) that the body exists, when one half of us tells us that it does, and it does no good to deny (with the modern, materialist sophisticate) that the mind exists, when you cannot prove it, and one half of us tells us that it does. On this last point, Descartes holds his ground. But no one has ever explained the connection of these two halves to us. There the matter rests and has always rested. Plato couldn't explain the connection. A true skeptical philosophy, skeptical on all counts, not on just half of them, is the helpmeet of theology, the mother of faith. For, like it or not, that is all that is left to us.

But is it? Is it *all* that is left to us? Have the efforts of the philosophers been a *total* failure? The paradoxical problem of mind and body, preventing penetration of itself, provides at the same time an axiom of any science of humanity. Ironically this axiom is the contrary of the one that Aristotle proposed for the *Metaphysics*. The law of contradiction (Gamma, iii) works, when applied to the world of onta, things with predicates, attributes, properties. But being *qua* being, on hE on, transcends that world, as Aristotle himself saw (Z, iv—vi, x) and as the neoplatonists subsequently stated more emphatically. Here Aristotle's law of contradiction does *not* apply, where there are no more attributes, and where everything is founded upon one ultimate contradiction that cannot be evaded. Even any lesser science that involves the interplay of mind and body, that is to say any science of humanity, any of what we today loosely call the social sciences, will have to recognize a new, revised and contradictory law of contradiction: to gar auto hama huparchein te kai mE huparchein anagkaion tOi autOi kai kata to auto. For any statement we may make, the contrary statement IS equally true. This strange axiom is going to require exploration. Meanwhile, practise proves that it works, and a search will reveal that there is already a considerable body of unselfconscious literature on the subject, by some who know this but seem not yet to know they know it. For the nonce the point to be made is that the *Metaphysics* has a present and a future context, as well as past ones.

Claremont, California,
December 12, 2001

0-595-21304-9